Chicken Stock Button Salt Pepper
White Wine
Mushrooms Sauce

Pottato Slieed Jesent
Red Wine ½ hour
Peeled onnion
Parsly Pepper

180
99 mins
Egg Wash.

Parsley
White wine
Onnions
Leeeks
Chicken
Mud ford
Green fro

Stones of Adoration

Sacred Stones and Mystic Megaliths of Ireland

For Guenter, with love...

Stones of Adoration

Sacred Stones and Mystic Megaliths of Ireland

CHRISTINE ZUCCHELLI

The Collins Press

Published in 2007 by

The Collins Press

West Link Park
Doughcloyne
Wilton
Cork

British Library Cataloguing in Publication Data
Zucchelli, Christine
    Stones of adoration : sacred stones & mystic megaliths
    of Ireland
    1. Sacred stones – Ireland 2. Megalithic monuments –
    Ireland 3. Folklore – Ireland 4. Ireland – Antiquities
    I. Title
    936.1'5

ISBN-13: 9781905172368

This publication has received support from the Heritage Council
under the 2007 Publications Grant Scheme

Book design and typesetting: Anú Design, Tara
Font: Bulmer 11.5 point
Printed in Malta

Contents

Acknowledgements

I wish to acknowledge with gratitude the assistance and help of all the people whom I approached during the preparation of this book. Writing about the folklore aspects of sacred stones would have been impossible without the support of the Department of Irish Folklore at University College Dublin; my heartfelt thanks to the head of the Department, Séamus Ó Catháin, for the permission to use the archive with its invaluable collections of Irish folklore, and to the full- and part-time collectors who have brought together such a wealth of different aspects of Irish folklore. I would also like to thank Patricia Lysaght and Dáithí Ó hÓgáin who are ever ready to share their vast knowledge and to give information and advice; to Bairbre Ní Fhloinn, Emer Ní Cheallaigh and Crístóir Mac Cárthaigh for their encouragement; and to Bo Almqvist, former head of the department, for introducing me to the fascinating world of sacred stones.

I wish to extend my gratitude to the staff at the library at University College Dublin, and to public libraries all over Ireland for kindly helping me locate written sources; for their constant assistance, my special thanks to the Local Studies Centre in Ennis, and to Clare County Libraries in Kilrush and Kilkee.

During my years of fieldwork, I have knocked on uncountable doors and asked for directions, information and permission to access stones that lie on private lands. I was overwhelmed by the kindness and helpfulness that I met throughout the country, and by the willingness of people to give their time and their stories. So many individuals have thus become involved in the making of this book that I could not begin to name them all. I must single out those who gave particular help: the late Gerry Cribbin,

Noel O'Neill and Michael Murphy (County Mayo), Peter Fallon (County Meath), Frank Gillespie (County Donegal), Chris Lawlor (County Wicklow), Laurence O'Donohue (County Cork), Ronan Quinn (County Armagh) and the staff of the Roe Valley Park (County Derry), who all went out of their way to help me with my research.

For helping to make this book a reality, I am much indebted to The Collins Press' editor Maria O'Donovan for her painstaking reading and re-reading of the typescript, for her patience and her invaluable advise and criticism. I must also thank Karen Carty and Terry Foley of Anú Design for taking so much trouble with the terrific design of the book and its cover.

Thanks also to John Kelly, photographer with the *Clare Champion*, Ennis, County Clare for his prompt support when I was at my wit's end with my knowledge of digital photography.

Last, but not least, to my husband Guenter, for believing in the project from the very start, and for his unfaltering support and the readiness to live for several years very intensely with the sacred stones of Ireland.

Introduction

One of the earliest references to the veneration of an individual stone in Ireland is a glossary to an Old Irish law tract. It dates back to the seventh or eighth century and gives a list of landmarks, among them a 'stone of adoration'. The writer did not reveal the nature of the stone; perhaps his mind was set on one of the numerous pre-historic monuments that dot the Irish landscape, or on a natural rock of conspicuous shape or size. Writing in the early medieval period, he might have thought a stone was considered 'adorable' for its Christian connotation.[1]

In numerous cultures all over the world, adorable or highly revered stones and stone monuments form integral parts of what we can describe as 'sacred landscapes'. Other prominent aspects of these spiritual landscapes would be sacred trees, waters, islands or mountains. The term sacred is used here to denote a spiritual or religious significance, and does not necessarily appear in its Christian understanding. Generally spoken, sacred features of the landscape come into being when humans acknowledge the presence of an *anima loci*, the spirit or the essence of a place. The nature of the *anima loci* is determined by the concept of beliefs that prevails within a society. With history being a continuous process of cultural development and change, the spiritual and religious concepts develop and change as well, and so does the definition of what is considered sacred for a particular reason. A perfect mirror for the changing perceptions of sacredness is folklore, because it is conservative by its nature yet also absorbs new ideas and influences from outside, and likewise adapts older ideas to new situations.

The earliest spiritual concept is the animistic tradition, which regards all natural features as spirited,

**Birr or Seffin Stone,
Birr, County Offaly**

*'Before cock crow thou wilt
thrice disown me', said Jesus
to Peter. It is commonly known
that the prophecy of Peter's
denial soon became true. Less
prominent is a tradition which
was current in nineteenth-
century Ennis and claimed
that the cock uttered his fatal
crow from a boulder on which
he left the imprints of his feet
as a testimony of his presence.
Miraculously, the stone had
travelled to Birr in County
Offaly, but around 1830 was
brought to Cullaun House near
Ennis in County Clare.*

*The Birr Stone has not always
been linked with Christian
traditions. About 1680, when
the boulder was still in Birr, it
was presented as the 'Navel of
Ireland' and thus associated
with the myth of the earth
goddess. A century later, the
conspicuous imprints in the
stone were interpreted in the
spirit of ancient heroic tales
and attributed to the giant
warrior Fionn mac Cumhaill.
Since 1974, when the boulder
was removed from Ennis to
Birr, it is again linked with
Fionn and his warriors.*[2]

J.J.W 1896

animated parts of the earth. Where the earth is seen as the body of her creator, natural features in the landscape are regarded as body parts of the creating earth mother or earth goddess. This concept predates formal religions, and would still surface in the oral tradition of stones that walk about or speak. When polytheistic religions emerged, the earth mother manifested herself in the shape of various goddesses; male deities appeared by their sides, usually presided over by a father god; sacred stones and stone monuments became interpreted as the homes of goddesses and gods. Monotheistic religions finally identify sacred sites as places chosen and blessed by members of the holy family, or by saints or prophets.

The body of Irish stone folklore that lies before us today is mainly aetiological, that is, explaining the origin of stones or stone monuments. The narratives reflect the spiritual world of pre-historic to early medieval Ireland, and are only slightly influenced by later impacts from outside. The main actors of legends and tales, however, are seen through the filter of Christian spirituality; hence, ancient goddesses survive in folklore as otherworld women, hags and fairies, the gods became mythical heroes and kings, or giants; and several deities were transformed into saints. In all these guises they would usually retain their link to their traditional sacred places. Alternatively, Christian legends would demonise the ancient deities, have them overpowered by the new faith and their places of worship taken over by saints.

From the seventh century, when the monasteries of the Celtic Church had become centres of education and literary traditions, clerics compiled biographies of saints, and historical or pseudo-historical tracts, annals and genealogies. For the first time, ancient oral lore and history were preserved in writing, and these writings provide the earliest sources for the veneration and folklore of stones in Ireland.

The composers of hagiographical texts drew their inspirations mainly from Biblical texts, especially from the Old and New Testaments, and from the Lives of continental saints, but they also included motives that were current in native Celtic lore. Even deeper steeped in ancient native traditions are myths, sagas and hero tales. The tales were initially orally transmitted, and many of them might have been current from the fourth century. They survive largely in manuscripts from the twelfth century, which were written more or less completely in the Irish language and had often been copied from older manu-scripts. Today, the ancient sagas and tales are conveniently grouped into four cycles of tales – the Mythological Cycle, the Ulster Cycle, the Fenian or Ossianic Cycle and the Historical Cycle or Cycle of the Kings.[3]

The Mythological Cycle of tales – though not acknowledged by historians as a reliable source of Irish pre-history – gives particular insight into the spiritual world of ancient Ireland, and provides the most valuable pieces of information on the earliest beliefs behind the sacred stones and stone monuments of the country. The core of the Mythological Cycle of tales is the *Leabhar Gabhála Éireann* or the Book of Invasions of Ireland, a compilation of pseudo-historical texts which reconstruct the conquest of the country by successive groups of peoples. The authors of such works as the *Leabhar Gabhála* were Christian monks; occasionally they even tried to establish a Biblical origin of the ancient Irish, and relate that it was Cessair, daughter or granddaughter of Noah, who led the first ever settlers to Ireland.[4] The *Leabhar Gabhála* itself begins with the story of Partholán and his sons. Coming from Greece, they arrived in Ireland after the Flood in about 2678 BC, and settled in the west. Centuries later, their descendants were wiped out by the plague. The people of Neimheadh, from Scythia, and his wife Macha were the next to appear in the country. They cultivated land in south Armagh, but were soon defeated and destroyed by the Formhóire or Formorians, who were either invaders or an already present earlier culture. Neimheadh's sons managed to escape to different parts of the world. Generations later, two rival branches of their descendants – the Fir Bolg and the Tuatha Dé Danann – should return. The Fir Bolg are said to have come from Greece; they divided Ireland into provinces and established the system of sacral kingship. On their arrival from Denmark or Greece – the myths differ on their provenance – the Tuatha Dé Danann or the People of the Goddess Danu fought and defeated the Fir Bolg and the Formorians, thus taking the sovereignty of Ireland. They had finally to submit to the Sons of Míl or Milesians, the ancestors of the present Celtic people, who came from Asia Minor and landed in the south west.[5]

The three remaining cycles are characteristically heroic and deal with the deeds of Celtic warriors and kings. Tales are set from around the time of the birth of Christ, but again many of their motifs, plots and characters seem to derive from earlier narrative traditions. They reflect particularly Celtic spirituality, and give insight into the role of sacred stones in an aristocratic warrior society.

The ancient myths and sagas, legends and biographies of saints were read out, and consequently various episodes from the literary tradition filtered back into folklore. From medieval times, Vikings, monastic orders from the Continent, Normans, English and Scottish settlers introduced motifs from their own spiritual worlds, but their ideas were largely absorbed into the native perceptions of otherworld women, heroes and saints as the divine characters behind sacred stones and stone monuments.

When people seek the divine at sacred places, when they communicate with the divine through certain rites and offerings, they recognise and reconfirm the sanctity of the location. Anciently, we have to understand these rites as ceremonies to please the divine, but as there are no written records from the customs in pre-Christian Ireland we depend on the biographies of Irish saints for the earliest information on the practical implementation of sacred stones in religious, social and spiritual affairs. The survival of archaic traits and elements as key parts of the rituals, however, indicate that some practices are considerably older then Christianity.

A prerequisite to release the indwelling powers and virtues of sacred stones is the physical contact between the applicant and the material. The act of literally connecting with the stone is an ancient trait

**Cursing Altar,
Inishmurray, County Sligo**

of contagious magic, based on the belief that the essence of spirits or people to which an object owns its virtues is still alive within that object. Likewise of ancient origin is the crucial importance of the direction of movement during the performance. In Ireland, as in many parts of the world, anticlockwise motions are considered unlucky, and only suitable for sorcery and destructive magic. Popularly referred to as left-hand-wise, widdershins or *tuafal*, they are usually applied in cursing rituals. Clockwise or sun-wise, also known as right-hand-wise or *deiseal*, is the appropriate movement for constructive magic and blessings, and subsequently reserved for healing and wishing.

The early Celtic Church, distinguished by her ability to adapt pagan ideas and reinterpret them in a Christian context, had no problems with incorporating older traits into her own complex of religious observances. Only from the twelfth century, when ecclesiastic reforms from the Continent had swept over to Ireland,[6] should the Church hierarchy change her attitude and begin to consider semi-pagan practices as superstitions. Monastic orders from the Continent were encouraged to settle in Ireland and to bring the Celtic Church spiritually and structurally in line with the principles of the Papacy. All over the country, stone churches and monasteries were built, usually in the Irish Romanesque style with its arched doorways and figural carvings. Replacing earlier timber structures and open-air altars, the churches should provide a venue for controlled and organised Christian observances. Whether it was desired by the orders or not, it seems that the cult of sacred stones was to a certain degree transferred or extended from sacred places in the landscape to the stone carvings in and about those new religious centres.

An even deeper influence on the role of sacred stones in folk customs and popular religion had the political and social development of the country from the late medieval period. In 1155, Pope Adrian IV – the only English pope in history – granted the sovereignty of Ireland to the Anglo-Norman king of England, Henry II. Justified as a tactical move to aid the process of Church reform and to copper-fasten the papal influence on spiritual matters in the country, it was practically a licence for the ensuing Norman and English conquests of Ireland. The authority of the Papacy in Ireland began to decrease considerably from the 1530s, when King Henry VIII had set up the independent Anglican Church – in Ireland established as the Church of Ireland – under the supremacy of the English monarch. The Reformed Church did not have the cultural insight nor the language for large-scale conversions; although declared the one and only official Church, she became the Church for those loyal to the English Crown, while wide sections of the native Irish population did not convert and held on to the Catholic faith.

Irish Catholicism in those days still held many elements and views of the early Celtic Church. On the Continent the Counter-Reformation, inspired by the Council of Trent (1545-1563), had widely succeeded in erasing semi-pagan practices from Catholic devotion. Papal attempts to modernise Catholicism in Ireland came to an abrupt end with Cromwell's offensive in 1649. The persecution of the Catholic faith under Cromwell's regime, followed by oppressive laws in the aftermath of the Battle of the Boyne at the end of the century, deprived the Catholic Church of the structure and means to effectively eliminate what it considered superstitious observations. At the same time, the political circumstances created an atmosphere that allowed magic practices to flourish, and Irish Catholicism developed an even deeper popular character with an eclectic mixture of orthodox and pagan elements. Often ridiculed by hostile contemporary observers, many of these archaic customs and traditions were, in fact, social and spiritual utilities created and fostered by oppression and poverty. In times of crisis or emotional unrest, people resorted to healing stones where no proper medical service was available, and to protective stones to find truth, justice and revenge when they could not trust the courts. Due to the destruction of Church property, Irish Catholics had none or few churches to attend, and Mass was often offered in private houses or at the ancient ceremonial places like holy wells and sacred stones.[7]

It was only after Catholic Emancipation in 1829, and especially after the Famine years in the 1840s, that the Church hierarchy in Ireland gained sufficient power to modernise herself and to rid Catholic devotion from unconventional archaic practices.

The leading figure of this reform was Paul Cullen, Archbishop of Armagh from 1840 to 1870. Determined to spiritually structure Irish Catholicism along the lines and principles of Rome, Cullen banned pilgrimages to holy wells, suppressed the celebration of Mass in private houses and at Mass Rocks, and ordered or encouraged the removal or destruction of several sacred stones. Under his supremacy, new churches were built, often of impressive dimensions. Aiding his intention to transform religious worship from outdoor affairs into well-organised public services in consecrated buildings,

**Doughnambraher,
Killeen, County Clare**

they were at the same time demonstrations of the rise and increasing power of the Catholic Church in Ireland.[8] Characteristically, there was a tendency to dedicate these new churches to the Virgin Mary rather than to a local patron saint. From the times of the Crusades, a passionate veneration of Mary has spread throughout western Christendom. On the Continent, encouraged by the Catholic Church, countless sacred places and chapels have since been re-dedicated, with Mary replacing the earlier patron saints. In Ireland, re-dedications are rather scarce; the love and devotion to the Virgin, however, is apparent in the erection of statues and Lourdes-style grottoes throughout the country, and in her intense veneration in the context of apparitions.

At about the same time, when older popular traditions and religious practices began to lose their significance in people's everyday lives, a rise of national sentiment and growing interest in the cultural heritage of the country became apparent among scholars from various disciplines. Antiquarian societies such as the Royal Irish Academy or The Royal Society of Antiquities in Ireland were founded to research archaeological, historical and folkloristic aspects of Irish culture. Their reports, together with the letters and memoirs of the Ordnance Survey, established in 1823, contributed significantly to the preservation and documentation of popular traditions. An invaluable source of information on all aspects of folklore is the manuscript collection of the Irish Folklore Commission in the Department of Irish Folklore at University College Dublin. The commission, established in 1927 as *An Cumann le Béaloideas Éireann* or the Irish Folklore Society, had focused on a systematic documentation of folk traditions and oral lore. Since 1956, the Ulster Folk and Transport Museum in Bangor is committed to illustrate and preserve the traditions of people in the North.

References regarding the practical use of stones are numerous in surveys, travellers' accounts and reports of antiquarians, and in the folklore collections of the Irish Folklore Commission. They give a lively picture of public performances in the context of pilgrimages and patterns, and of rather private observances at healing, swearing, wishing and cursing stones. The most detailed data relate to the period from the early nineteenth to the early decades of the twentieth century and show that, in spite of a certain decline due to the suppressive measures in the course of Cullen's Church reform, most of these practices continued at least into the middle of the last century. With the rapid urbanisation, modernisation and industrialisation of Irish society throughout the last decades, the old popular traditions came again under serious threat. Fortunately, there are clear indications that they are not entirely lost and gone.

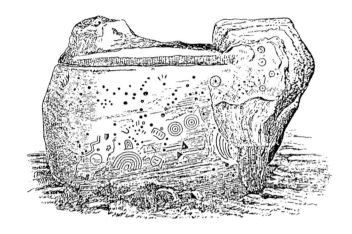

PART I

Origins — Myths, Legends, Folklore

Goddess, Hags and Fairy Queens

Facing northward, and set about four feet inwards from the circumference of one of the largest and most conspicuous carns [sic] which crown the Loughcrew Hills, there is a huge boulder, weighing about ten tons, and popularly called 'the Hag's Chair'. The name is derived from Vera, the celebrated goddess, sorceress, or hag, of ancient days.

Wood-Martin, *Traces of the Elder Faiths in Ireland* (1902)[1]

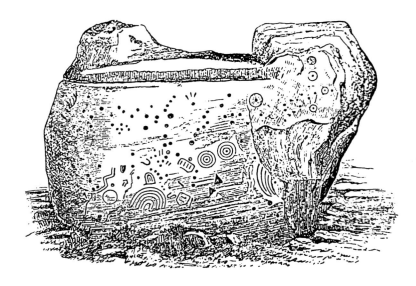

**The Hag's Chair,
Loughcrew, County Meath**

At a first glance, the individual female characters that are popularly linked with sacred stones seem to belong to entirely different bodies of narratives. A closer look, however, reveals that the vast majority of them have their roots in the ancient concept of an earth goddess or mother goddess. The cult of the earth goddess is commonly associated with ancient matrifocal societies. It is a worldwide phenomenon, with its origin apparently reaching back into the earliest days of human existence. The goddess is understood as the life-giving force and at the same time as the reaper, embodying the cycle of birth, death and regeneration. She is the creator of the earth, and the earth is seen as her body. Mountains and hills are taken for her belly and breasts, caves for her womb and pillars for her navel.

The beginning of a goddess cult in Ireland is not undisputed. Some scholars claim, that her veneration developed only after the Indo-European conquest, when a formal religion had emerged. Others suggest convincingly that the earth goddess initially belonged to the Neolithic or New Stone Age, when society became essentially agricultural and must have been especially concerned with the fertility of livestock and crops.

Very little is known about Ireland's earliest farmers, who arrived probably around 4,000 BC. They brought cereals with them that were native to the east Mediterranean, and the knowledge to cultivate grains and domesticate animals.[2]

The sagas of ancient Ireland attribute the introduction of different agricultural means and methods to the leaders of the first groups of peoples who settled in the country: Cessair, so the myths say, brought sheep with her from the land of the Bible; Partholán, coming from Greece, cleared plains in the west for the first cattle in Ireland; his sons introduced the art of brewing, presumably together with the grains required for the process; Neimheadh and his family cultivated pastures in the north.

Archaeologists and historians too suggest that separate groups of people settled in Ireland during the Neolithic period. They would have come from Atlantic Europe, and – from about 3,800 BC – began to construct massive stone monuments which were previously unknown in Ireland. The structures are called megaliths or megalithic monuments, from the Greek terms *mega* for large and *lithos* for stone; owing to the finds of human remains within them, they are commonly labelled tombs or graves.

Scholars reckon that the growing importance of fertile land, combined with the cult of the ancestors who took possession of a territory, had initiated the development of megaliths. They would have been designed as perpetual houses for the dead or, in a spiritual sense, as permanent reminders of the presence of the ancestors' souls; often built in commanding situations, they might have served as territorial markers, stressing the claim of a community over the lands which their ancestors had cultivated. About 1,200 examples survive into our day; their different layouts allow identifying four basic types, namely court cairns, portal tombs, passage graves, and – a final variant from the late Neolithic and early Bronze Age – wedge tombs. The types of megalithic structures overlap in the time of construction and use, and to a certain degree in their regional distribution, and were presumably introduced by different population groups.[3]

There are indications, however, that the monuments were not merely graves or manifestations of an ancestral cult, but likewise assembly sites for rituals and ceremonies. The characteristic circular or semi-circular enclosures at the entrance to court cairns, in particular, suggest a ritual designation. The frequent orientation of megaliths towards the east points to a reverence for the sun and her association with growth and fecundity. This link is especially obvious at passage graves, with small fertility symbols found inside the chambers and chiselled into structural stones, and their layout in the shape of human bodies. Accepting the monuments of the Stone Age as combined centres of ceremonial worship and burial, we can compare them to the cathedrals and churches of modern Europe, with their tombs and sarcophagi of important people.

It is amazing to note to which extent Irish folk tradition – and indeed oral lore throughout the distribution area of megaliths in Europe – has preserved the association of megaliths with fertility. Narratives would primarily link those ancient monuments to several later emanations of the earth goddess, and explain them as divine abodes, seats, beds or final resting places; the custom of harvest celebrations and fertility rites at those sites survived well into the twentieth century.

The transformation of a matrifocal society, with its veneration of the earth goddess, into a patriarchal culture, with a rather structured polytheistic religion, began with the infiltration of Indo-European peoples during the Bronze Age, and was continued by the Celtic conquest in the subsequent Iron Age. Reflections of the disempowerment of the earth goddess appear in myths, medieval literature and folklore.

The *Dindshenchas*, a twelfth-century collection of older poems and prose tales which explain the place-names of Ireland, would repeatedly refer to ancient goddesses who had to submit to invading warriors of the metal ages; some were raped, or compelled to marry their conquerors, whilst others died through acts of male villainy. Tailtiu of the Fir Bolg was forced to clear forests until she died of exhaustion; Tlachtga was raped by a gang of Milesians and died when she came down with three sons by three fathers in one birth. Macha was pregnant when she had to run a race in Eamhain Mhacha against the horses of King Conchobhar mac Nessa; she died after giving birth to twins.[4] In folklore this conflict is animatedly recalled in the lore of the violent relationship between otherworld women and their heroic lovers or husbands.

The violence broke the superiority of the earth goddess, and hence enabled her absorption into the Indo-European concepts of tutelary goddesses and divine mothers of other deities. Her former cult centres, remembered as the sites of her defeat and often named after her, would frequently become the political or ceremonial centres of the conquerors. Split up into different territorial goddesses, the earth mother continued to guard over the prosperity and fertility of the land, and often over her descendants which sprang from the union with her captor. In Celtic spirituality the goddess of the land appears as the embodiment of sovereignty, who had to accept a prospective chieftain or king to make his reign legitimate and prolific for his people.

The Celtic perception of the goddess as the mythical ancestress survived in popular tradition and is still prevalent in the lore of the banshee, the death messenger of distinctive Gaelic clans. In the later medieval period, Anglo-Normans adopted the concept, and transformed it into the idea of a super-natural mermaid-ancestress.

Folklore and medieval literature preserve also the memory of land goddesses. Some appear in the shape of otherworld ladies or fairies; others are remembered under individual names. The most common

The White Stone of Calliagh Beri, Dorsey, County Armagh

South-Armagh traditions link the theme of the power struggle between goddess and hero with the Cailleach Bhéarra and the warrior Fionn mac Cumhaill. Several pillar stones in the Slieve Gullion area are said to have been cast at each other by the lovers, and curious indentations on the stones are popularly explained as the fingerprints of the otherworld woman or the hero. One of their stone devices is the Long Stone on Carnhill, an ancient assembly site for harvest festivals on Bilberry Sunday at Mullyash in County Monaghan, about 10 miles from Slieve Gullion. Another magnificent example is the White Stone of Calliagh Beri near the Dorsey ramparts in County Armagh. The name recalls the custom to white-wash the pillar every year in spring time, though the practice was abolished in the early decades of the twentieth century.[5]

The Witch on the Wall, Fethard, County Tipperary

The duality of the goddess, the combination of old age and regeneration within herself, is beautifully illustrated in the carvings of Sheela-na-Gigs, which appear from the seventh century onwards. A powerful representation of this duality is the Sheela on the fourteenth-century town wall of Fethard in County Tipperary. Fethard lies in the shadow of Slievenamon, traditionally the main abode of the women of the otherworld.[6]

characters with regards to the lore of stones and ancient stone monuments are the Cailleach Bhéarra and Áine. It is possible that they have gradually taken over sites which formerly belonged to other land goddesses. Their names might likewise have been applied as a sort of codename to avoid mentioning the real name of the deity, comparable to the reluctance to refer to the fairies by their name. In the true tradition of the ancient goddess, both women materialise in different manifestations, changing their appearance from old to young, from ugly to beautiful, thus perfectly representing the cycle of life, death and recreation. Áine seems to personify primarily the bright aspect of the goddess, and would often be described as a young fairy lady or fairy queen. The lore of the Cailleach is more likely to focus on her dark side, subsequently – especially in the English language – she is recurrently depicted as an old hag or witch. Her frequent link with features of the physical landscape, or with pre-Celtic burial structures, and her association with different aspects of harvesting, connect the Cailleach with the myth of the earth mother. When she appears as a mythical clan ancestress or represents sovereignty, she stands obviously in the Celtic tradition.[7]

With the introduction of Christianity the perception of ancient deities inevitably underwent a significant change. While the hag or witch began to feature as an opponent to the new faith, some traits of the bright, productive aspect of the goddess were considered compatible to Christian principles. As a result, several female saints inherited the divine link to fertility and healing, to sacred stones, trees and wells. As we will see in the context of Christian stone lore, it was particularly Saint Brigid who took over ritual sites and cultic elements from the goddess.

The Stone Navel of Éire

'They found [Ireland] uninhabited and divided it in five equal portions among themselves. The bounds of these divisions meet at a certain stone in Meath near the Castle of Kilair. This stone is said to be the navel of Ireland, as it were, placed right in the middle of the land. Consequently that part of Ireland is called Meath, as being situated in the middle of the island.'[8]

Giraldus Cambrensis, in his twelfth-century account of the *History and Topography of Ireland,* refers to the Stone of Divisions on the Hill of Uisneach in County Westmeath and the mythical division of the country among the five brothers who led the Fir Bolg on their conquest of Ireland. The Navel of Ireland is almost 20 feet high and estimated to weigh over 30 tons. It has five ridges, said to represent the five ancient provinces of Ireland. An ancient five-fold division of the country is accepted by historians, and commemorated in the Irish term for a province, *cúige*, a fifth.

A sixth-century poem in the Middle Irish text on 'The Settling of the Manor of Tara' suggests that the significance of the conspicuous erratic boulder dates back into the earliest times of human activity in Ireland. The poem is attributed to the fictional Fintan, husband of Cessair and only survivor of the Flood, who lived in different shapes into early Christian times. Fintan recalls the past and claims that 'It is long since I drank a drink of the Deluge over the Navel of Uisneach'.[9]

Oval or dome-shaped central pillars were especially popular among societies near the Mediterranean. Archaeologists recorded the earliest stones of that type in Palestine; but the most famous example which should give its Greek name to that particular type of pillars is certainly the *omphalos* or 'Navel of the World' in the ruined sanctuary of Delphi. The omphalos tradition is based on the notion of the human navel as the source of human life. Spiritually, this concept translates into the earth being born from the navel of a mother goddess; the omphalos stone as the symbolic

Castlestrange, County Roscommon (left) **and Turoe, Bullaun, County Galway**

Archaeologists date the Castlestrange Stone to the third or second century BC and assign it to the Celtic Iron Age. The magnificent egg-shaped pillar is decorated all over with the characteristic curvilinear patterns of the Continental La Tène Celts. Four more pillars or fragments of stones with similar decorations have been discovered in Ireland since 1938. The Turoe Stone has been unearthed near a ring fort at Feerwore, a few kilometres from its present situation. The granite boulder had been roughly trimmed into its cylindrical shape, and could have been of omphallic or phallic symbolism. The decorations in the upper part of the pillar resemble those on the Castlestrange Stone but they are smaller and were partly executed by chiselling away the background, thus leaving the design in low relief.[10]

The Stone Navel of Ireland, or Aill na Míreann, the Stone of Divisions, Hill of Uisneach, County Westmeath

From the Leabhar Gabhála we learn that the Hill of Uisneach was linked to the queen and land goddess Éire and her sisters or manifestations Banba and Fódla. The Tuatha Dé Danann ladies were dis-empowered by three leaders of the Milesians, but consented to marry them under the condition that their names remain on the country forever. The effect of the promise reaches into our days, with poetry and literature often using Banba and Fódla as synonyms for the country, while Éire is the name of Ireland in the Irish language. Consequently, we can assume that the navel stone of Ireland was anciently understood as the stone navel of the goddess Éire.[11]

representation of the divine navel would allow a spiritual connection to the goddess through certain ceremonies.[12]

The principle of a navel stone certainly predates the arrival of Celtic peoples in Ireland; material evidence, however, indicates that early Celts had adapted the concept into their own spiritual world, probably along with their preference for phallic shaped central stones.[13]

Hilltop Cairns — Homes of the Goddess

A twelfth-century text indicates that following their defeat, the Tuatha Dé Danann reached an agreement with the victorious Celtic Milesians. The truce allowed the Tuatha to stay in Ireland under the condition that they would take residence in the underworld and leave the upper part of the country to the Gaelic people. Thus, the gods and goddesses retreated into pre-historic cairns, mounds and barrows.[14]

The medieval text is considered an explanation of the much older belief of ancient monuments being the dwelling places of deities or spirits of the dead. In the literary tradition, the underworld dwellers can be either gender; in folklore, particularly in the lore of hilltop cairns, the emphasis lies clearly on female characters. Even in the contexts of heroic tales, where cairns are occasionally shown as the abodes or graves of warriors or male deities, the structures would primarily be understood to be the home of the otherworld lover or mother of the respective character, and only her permission would enable a hero to enter her abodes.

The most recurrent character in the aetiological lore of Neolithic cairns is the Cailleach Bhéarra in her aspect as a land goddess, or as a 'shaper of the landscape'. Her name appears in different regional variations, from Calliagh Beri or Cally Berry to Waura or Vera; sometimes she is merely the Cailleach, the hag, the witch or the old lady.

One central motif is the Cailleach carrying an apron full of stones. They would eventually fall from the apron and thus form cairns on mountain tops. Place-names, for instance Carnberí in County Louth, preserve the memory of the tale. The narrative spread eastwards, and variants have been recorded in Wales, England and Scotland.[15]

Slievenamon, the Mountain of the Women, County Tipperary

Where the individual names of deities are lost, folk memory would often refer to them as fairies or sídhe. Sídhe means literally 'mounds' and is a reference to the homes of the otherworld communities. When linked with cairns, fairies would commonly be thought of as female characters. They are believed to have their main residence in the cairn on top of Slievenamon or Sliabh na mBan in County Tipperary, and to inhabit numerous other tumuli in the country.[16]

The Hag's Cairn, Loughcrew, County Meath

The 'Caillaigh Waura' could have ruled the country, so the story goes, if she had managed to jump with an apron full of stones between the hilltops at Loughcrew. To her disappointment she dropped a handful of stones on the first hill, and some more on the second; infuriated she emptied her apron on the third hill. The piles of stones remained where they were, forming the hilltop cairns of Slieve na Cailligh. The Cailleach herself retreated into the cairn on the central hill; the decorated stone that forms part of its kerb is her seat, the Hag's Chair, from where she looks out over the land that she has lost.[17]

In Ulster folklore, the Cailleach's home is set on Slieve Gullion; from her abode in the chamber beneath the southern cairn – locally known as Cailleach Berra's House or the Old Lady's House – she watches over the prosperity of her territory. Throughout the country, we find several Neolithic structures which are popularly dubbed the houses or beds of 'the hag' or 'the old woman', and it is safe to assume that the majority of them belonged initially to the Cailleach.[18]

Passage Tombs — Graves of Mythical Queens

As discussed there is a strong link between cairns – especially those on hilltops – and ancient goddesses of the land. Being representatives of the perpetual cycle of life, death and recreation, the goddesses were understood to be immortal. Even when a tale featured a goddess overpowered or killed, she would only withdraw for a while before re-emerging in her former glory. Consequently, a goddess would not require a grave or tomb, and hilltop cairns could only be considered her permanent or temporary dwellings. The situation is different where folk memory had transformed the perception of an ancient goddess and transported her from a mythical into an historical context. The goddess would then appear as a pseudo-historical character, usually a queen, with her cairn regarded as her final resting place rather than her home.

The best-known example of such a transformation is certainly the cairn on Knocknarea in County Sligo. Popular tradition insists that the cairn is the burial place of the Connacht queen Meadhbh, who reigned in the first century AD. She was the warrior queen who – contesting her husband Ailill over the equality of their wealth- initiated the Táin Bó Cuailnge, the Cattle Raid of Cooley, and subsequently the war between the provinces of Connacht and Ulster. It is still a matter of controversy whether Queen Meadhbh was a historical character or a medieval literary derivation of a mythical land goddess, and as such related to the goddess of sovereignty, Medb Lethderg, whose consent was required to gain the kingship of Tara. In the lore of Sligo, irrespective of her designation as an historical queen, she stands clearly in the tradition as an immortal goddess of the land.

Meadhbh's Grave has never been excavated but archaeologists reckon that it contains a Neolithic passage grave, with a stone passage leading into an inner chamber near or at the centre of the cairn. It is estimated that 300 of these structures survived in Ireland, characteristically covered by round cairns

Meadhbh's Grave (Meascán Méidhbh), Knocknarea, County Sligo
(Opposite page)

Standing upright, so she can oversee her former realm – that is how Queen Meadhbh is allegedly buried under the cairn on the summit of Knocknarea. Others claim that her eyes are turned towards Ulster, waiting for a chance to avenge the defeat of Connacht in the aftermath of the Cattle Raid of Cooley. Meadhbh's Cairn – sometimes locally referred to as Meadhbh's Lump – is massive, measuring c. 630 feet in circumference, 35 feet in height, and consisting of an estimated 40,000 stones. Still, anyone climbing to the hilltop would add another stone in order to have a wish granted or, according to older traditions, to prevent Meadhbh from ever emerging from under the cairn again. Nevertheless, once in seven years a female apparition would haunt Knocknarea and woe to the person who meets her.[19]

and grouped into cemeteries on neighbouring hilltops or elevated places. The passage grave builders arrived from Atlantic Europe, maybe from Brittany, and landed either near the mouth of the river Boyne, or in the west near present-day Sligo. Along a diagonal line connecting the Boyne Valley with Sligo, they established the most significant and impressive passage grave cemeteries of the country. It is interesting to note that in the tradition of the Boyne monuments we meet again a goddess with strong links to cattle, namely Bóinn, the white cow goddess.[20]

Decorated Kerbstone, Newgrange, County Meath

We do not know much about the people of the passage grave culture; even their arrival in Ireland is uncertain and has been dated to different times between 3,300 and 2,500 BC. Archaeological evidence, however, points to a worship of the sun and possibly to the moon; a ritual function of the stone structures with regards to fertility and growth is indicated by the deposits of fertility symbols as small balls of stone or chalk, or decorated stone phalli inside the chambers.[21]

The high reverence for the sun is apparent in the alignment of many passages to sunrise or sunset on the summer or winter solstices, the longest and shortest days of the year respectively, or at spring or autumn equinoxes, the days and nights of equal length; at Newgrange the sunshine reaches the chamber exclusively around the winter solstice; at Knowth the passage is found to align to the rising and setting sun on the spring and autumn equinoxes.[22]

In several places, particularly at Newgrange, Loughcrew and Knowth, all in County Meath, and at Baltinglass in County Wicklow, the builders used considerable quantities of quartz to decorate the face or outer walls of the mounds.[23] Spiritually, the white crystalline stone is sometimes connected with the rising sun; more commonly, however, it is linked with the moon and the female cycle. Inside the cairns, the colour red occurs conspicuously often, be it as red sandstone slabs, or red ochre for the decorations. Red is associated with blood and birth, and appears frequently together with notions of the earth mother. The chambers themselves have sometimes been compared to her divine womb, suggesting that the passage graves were in fact a further development of the sacred natural caves which earlier cultures abroad had honoured as the womb of the earth mother or great goddess. A remarkable discovery, noted at several passage graves in Ireland and clearly supporting the idea that the builders had actually intended to re-create the body of the goddess, is the fact that the large internal stones of passage and chambers were arranged forming the outline of a human body.

Another peculiarity of passage graves in Ireland and Brittany are decorations picked on structural stones within, or on kerbstones around their cairns. Although formally known as passage grave art, the ornamentations were certainly more than just artistic decorations, and the recurrent use of a few central motifs indicate a magic or cultic connotation.

The most common motifs are spirals, which are generally taken as symbols of the constant flow of energy and the cycle of life, and accordingly for representations of the earth goddess; concentric circles and cup-marks, widely believed to symbolise the sun, or else the navel from which all life comes; zigzag lines standing for water; triangles and serpentine lines, again represent the earth mother.[24]

The Grave of Queen Baine, Knockmany Hill, County Tyrone

An entry in the Annals of the Four Masters for the year 111 AD records the death of Queen Baine, mother of Feidhlimidh Reachtmhar, son of Tuathal Teachtmhar, and her internment at 'Cnoc-Baine in Oirghialla'. As with Queen Meadhbh from Connacht, the identity of Baine is doubtful, and she seems to be a mythical rather than an historical character. According to the folklore of the area Baine was a local queen; upon her own wish she was buried on Knockmany Hill in an already existing passage grave. Its chamber, formed by beautifully carved reddish sandstone slabs, was traditionally considered the home of a fairy woman named Anya, an emanation of Danu or Ana, the mother goddess of the Tuatha Dé Danann.[25]

The Hag's Cairn, Loughcrew, County Meath

Loughcrew belongs firmly and inseparably to the Cailleach Bhéarra, and the largest of the cairns, with its lavishly decorated stones, is generally described as her dwelling place. Throughout the nineteenth century, several scholars attempted to establish the initial significance of the Neolithic cemetery, and suggested that the Hag's Cairn might have been the tomb of Ollamh Fodhla, the legendary king and first law-giver of Ireland, or the grave of the mythical queen, Tailtiu. The vague local tradition which describes the cairn as the grave of the Cailleach has probably derived from one of these theories.[26]

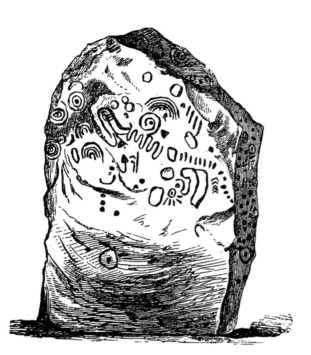
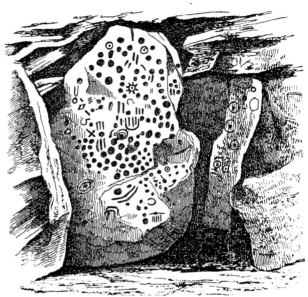

Beds of Stone for Old Hag and Fair Maiden

The tradition of gigantic stone beds built by or for mythical female characters is particularly popular in the west of Ireland. In folklore and place-names, those beds would often appear as 'labby' or in similar anglicised versions of the Irish word *leaba* for a bed. In archaeological terms, the stone beds would usually be portal tombs or wedge cairns.

Wedge tombs, or wedge-shaped gallery graves, were built around 2,000 BC, during the transitional period between late Neolithic and early Bronze Age. Some 400 have been identified today, predominately in the west. Portal tombs are earlier; they belong to the Stone Age, and were probably contemporary with the hilltop cairns of passage graves. These magnificent structures are commonly and fittingly dubbed dolmens, from the Breton word for a stone table; the Irish term for a dolmen is *cromleac*, a stooped stone. About 160 dolmens survived in Ireland, and examples occur in almost every county.[27] The striking appearance of the monuments captivated the attention of eighteenth- and nineteenth-century antiquarians, who would regularly attribute their construction to Celtic druids. In 1841, Mr and Mrs Hall corroborated such theories when they erroneously translated the term *cromleac* for 'Stone of Crom', and consequently interpreted dolmens as druidical altars for the worship of the pagan deity Crom Dubh or Crom Cruach.[28] In the folklore of dolmens and wedge cairns, however, druids and pagan worship have no place. In the north and east, their construction would characteristically be attributed to the giant hero, Fionn mac Cumhaill, and his warriors or to other anonymous giants, who built them for graves, griddle stones or tables. In the popular lore of the south west, they are more likely to appear as the stone beds of the Cailleach Bhéarra in her manifestation as an old hag; tradition in the mid-west finally would almost invariably take dolmens, and to a smaller extent wedge cairns, for the 'Beds of Diarmaid and Gráinne', recalling the lovers from the greatest tale within the Fenian lore, 'The Pursuit of Diarmaid and Gráinne'.

The tale was current from the ninth century onwards, but there are strong indications that the medieval writers had based the leading literary characters on the memory of ancient deities: when they refer to Diarmaid as Diarmaid Donn, they recall the underworld deity Donn; Donn's rival, Fionn, seems to be a medieval emanation of the mythical seer Find and the Celtic or Indo-European god Vindos.[29]

Gráinne means literally 'the ugly one', but she is consistently portrayed as a beautiful young woman, thus reflecting the dual aspects of the goddess. Her character appears to derive from the sun goddess Grian who was particularly venerated in County Clare and east County Limerick. With the frequent orientation of dolmens towards the rising sun, it is easy to imagine that a sun goddess had once been linked to the structures.[30] Place-names, for instance, like Carngraney, or Cairn of the Sun for a dolmen near Roughfort in County Antrim, show that this association exceeds the areas where the Diarmaid and Gráinne story is attached to dolmens. In the nineteenth century, women who had difficulties conceiving used to sleep on the 'Beds of Diarmaid and Gráinne', thus preserving the ancient fertility-promoting aspect of the sun goddess.

**The Bed of Diarmaid
and Gráinne, Cleenragh,
County Longford**

*The romance relates that
Gráinne, daughter of King
Cormac mac Airt, consented
to marry the ageing Fionn
mac Cumhaill. During their
engagement celebrations,
however, she fell in love with
the young Fianna hero,
Diarmaid, and persuaded him
to elope with her. For years,
Fionn pursued the lovers, until
he finally allowed them to settle
in the west. Popular tradition
developed the idea of the
lovers' flight, and tells of how
they ran from Fionn for the
duration of one year, building a
new bed of stones every night.* [31]

Labbacallee, Glanworth, County Cork

Labbacallee, or the 'Hag's Bed', is the largest wedge cairn in Ireland. It is dated to the transitional period when the myth of the Bronze Age warrior began to diminish the sole reign of the Neolithic earth goddess. Folklore reflects this struggle in the tales about the Cailleach Bhéarra's hostility towards her husbands. Here, around Glanworth, she is married to the druid Mogh Ruith, and a boulder in the river, down from the Labbacallee, is identified as a device which she had once cast at him.[32]

Rock Chairs and the Women of the Otherworld

Natural boulders or slightly modified stones in the shapes of seats are often popularly known as wishing chairs; trusted to fulfil any type of wish, they were once especially resorted to by women wishing to marry or to conceive. Many wishing chairs belong to the assembly sites of the ancient harvest festival of Lughnasa, and were, together with the festival, taken over by St Patrick, or, less frequently by St Brigid. Others – not necessarily regarded as wishing chairs – did not experience a Christian transformation, but retained their link to female deities and their medieval emanations.

St Brigid's Chair, Lough Derg, County Donegal

In 1835, the scholar John O'Donovan described the stone seat as St Daveaog's Chair and noted the 'oral tradition, which maintained that Daveaog was a woman who died during the turas, or pilgrimage walk, and was revived by St Patrick'. Having reached the rock called her chair, she died again and was interred on Saint's Island. Apart from the story given to O'Donovan, and a faint local tradition of St Patrick placing the converted community under the care of a fellow saint when he left the area, nothing is known about St Daveaog, and her chair has long been signed over to St Brigid. Daveaog may have been a local saint, who perhaps emanated from an earlier goddess of the area. Prior to St Patrick's arrival, Lough Derg belonged to the Caoranach or Corra, a spirit or dark manifestation of a goddess, who took on the shape of a serpent when she resided in the lake. Local tradition relates that she had swallowed St Patrick but the saint cut her open, and left her petrified serpent body in Lough Derg.[33]

The Hag's Chairs

As with the hilltop cairns the Cailleach Bhéarra plays a prominent role with regards to stone chairs. In the north, where passage tombs occur, her seats would often stand in the vicinity of these Neolithic structures. A splendid rock chair of the Cailleach is the decorated kerbstone at the main cairn at Loughcrew, County Meath. In a place called 'The Spellick', not far from her home on Slieve Gullion in County Armagh, she has another stone seat. Until the early decades of the twentieth century, communal harvest gatherings took place at the Spellick on Bilberry Sunday, and people would sit in the chair as part of the festivities.[34]

The Hag's Chair, Loughcrew, County Meath

In 1872, when Eugene Conwell associated Loughcrew with the legendary law-giver Ollamh Fodhla, he re-named the chair-shaped stone 'Ollamh Fodhla's Throne'. His proposal, along with the identification of Loughcrew with Teltown, as suggested by other nineteenth-century commentators, had little influence on local tradition. Their ideas should only occasionally emerge in accounts from the 1930s, which mention that 'Queen Tailte and Queen Maeve' sat on the rock to proclaim their laws to the people. Generally, however, the Hag's Chair belongs to the Cailleach Bhéarra, and is still treasured as a wishing chair.[35]

In the lore of west Munster, the Cailleach is particularly associated with the Beara Peninsula in County Cork. She has been regarded as mother or foster-mother to the ancestors of several leading clans, for instance the Corca Dhuibhne and the Corca Loighdhe, and numerous prehistoric monuments or natural features are assigned to her, among them a natural boulder near Kilcatherine Point, which some say is her petrified self, while others claim it is her chair where she sits and awaits her consort, Manannán mac Lir the god of the sea.[36]

Áine's Rock Chairs

In the east of the country, medieval literature and popular tradition associate the goddess Áine with Manannán mac Lir, and show her alternatively as his daughter or his wife. An allusion of Áine's relation to the sea survived until the nineteenth century in the oral lore at Dunany (*Dun Áine*) in County Louth, where a chair-shaped stone on the seashore was pointed out as *Cathaoir Ana* or Ana's Chair. The weekend after Lughnasa was considered sacred, and no ships would go out on these days in the honour of Áine and Manannán. More recently, the stone seat became known as the 'Madman's Chair', deriving from the notion that mad people would instinctively go and sit on it. From then on, their mental status would never change for the worse or better.[37]

Áine is closely related to Danu or Ana, the principle goddess of the Tuatha Dé Danann. The Paps of Anu, a group of hills shaped like breasts and a rounded belly in County Kerry, imply her veneration as an earth goddess, though on the Continent Danu is linked to water, and her memory is preserved in the names of rivers like the Danube. Aspects of Danu have passed into Irish folklore and medieval literature, and emerged in the form of several otherworld women called Áine. Her name means literally brightness or heat, suggesting that one aspect of the goddess was linked with the veneration of the sun. The nineteenth-century midsummer festivals at Knockainey, Áine's hill, in County Limerick, where celebrants lit bundles of straw and scattered them in the fields and among the animals to secure fertility and prosperity, may have been an echo of that ancient link. But popular tradition also preserves the memory of Áine as a Celtic goddess of sovereignty and a mystical otherworld ancestress to leading clans or families. The Eóganacht sept, for instance, who held the kingship of Munster from early historic times until the end of the tenth century, claimed their descent from Áine, who represented the sovereignty of Munster and was raped by the mythical founder of the clan.[38] In the fourteenth century,

**Suideachan –
The Housekeeper's Chair,
Lough Gur,
County Limerick**

Folk tradition adopted the Geraldine lore of Áine and relates that Gearóid Iarla's father seized her cloak when he saw her bathing in Lough Gur. Thus winning power over the otherworld woman, he fathered a son, Gearóid. In the early years of the twentieth century, a limestone rock at the shore of Lough Gur was still known as the Suideachan or the Housekeeper's Chair, and folklore accounts recall that several local men spotted beautiful Áine sitting on the stone and combing her hair with a golden comb. Encounters with Áine, however, were considered unlucky, and the unfortunate men lost their senses or died soon after their experience. Today, the link of the stone seat with Áine is almost entirely lost.[39]

the Geraldines were the leading Norman family in Ireland. Gearóid Iarla, Earl of Desmond, who led their Munster branch, successfully assimilated all aspects of Gaelic ways of life. It is very likely that he himself initiated the lore of his own descent from the Gaelic goddess Áine to stress the legitimacy of the Geraldine control of Munster.

The Banshee's Chairs

A folklore account from the 1930s reads: 'In a rock at the Corby Rock Mill [outside Monaghan town] there is a square seat carved in the rock and before anyone dies in the neighbourhood a banshee sits in the stone and cries: This stone is called the Banshee's Chair.'

Banshee or *badhbh* are the most frequent names for the female supernatural death messenger in Irish folk tradition. She is exclusively associated with distinctive Gaelic families, and believed to indicate the imminent death of a family member by crying in the way a human woman would keen. Accordingly,

The Banshee's Chairs, Ballinasilogue, County Carlow (opposite page) **and Modeligo, County Waterford** (right)

A rude stone seat in the Modeligo area was formerly pointed out as the Banshee's Chair; today it is only remembered as the 'Witch's Chair'. The Banshee Stone at Ballinasilogue in County Carlow – locally still regarded with respect – is a partly collapsed portal dolmen; the Bow Stone at Patrickswell, in the same county, is a wedge-shaped rock near the holy well.[40]

Carraig Chlíodhna, Kilshannig, County Cork

Another seat of Clíodhna, and at the same time her abode and entrance to the otherworld, is Carraig Chlíodhna near the County Cork village of Kilshannig. Here, she appears as the otherworld ancestress of the O'Keeffe family. A local legend tells that Clíodhna was in love with her sister's fiancée, a young O'Keeffe chieftain, and asked her to break the engagement off. When the sister refused that request, Clíodhna turned her into a cat, and could subsequently win the unsuspecting O'Keeffe for herself. They married and had a child, but the husband eventually learned of Clíodhna's deceit. He banished her forever, and Clíodhna chose to retreat to the conspicuous rock near Kilshannig.

she also appears as *bean chaointe* or *badhbh chaointe*. The concept of the banshee or *badhbh* as the death messengers of Gaelic families has developed from the ancient Celtic perception of a goddess of the land and of sovereignty as a tutelary otherworld ancestress. The motif of her explicit denial to foreigners was in all probability introduced as a result of the land seizures and confiscations during the sixteenth and seventeenth centuries. Her manifestations are generally aural rather than visual, except for the eastern parts of the country. Occasionally, when she appears, she does so in the true tradition of otherworld women – sitting on rough chairs of stone.

Several septs and families throughout the country have preserved the individual names of their banshees. Áine from Cnoc Aine at Lissan in County Derry, for instance, is attached to the local Corr family and would wail whenever one of them is about to die. Clíodhna or Cleena is the Callaheenacladdig, the Little Hag of the Sea from Ahaglaslin in County Cork, who sits and cries from a wedge cairn to announce the imminent death of anyone in the neighbourhood.[41]

The Children of the Mermaid

Entries in the annals of Ireland indicate that throughout medieval times the existence of mermaids was accepted as historical fact. The Annals of the Four Masters tell of how fishermen captured the mermaid, Liban, off the Antrim coast in 558 AD. For 1118, the Annals of the Four Masters note that fishermen have again discovered mermaids, this time in the Nore River in County Kilkenny, and near the town of Waterford.[42]

The motif of mermaids marrying mortal men though is an Irish adaptation of the Continental tale complex of the 'seal woman' or 'swan-woman', which arrived in Ireland only with the Anglo-Norman conquest of the twelfth century. The first Anglo-Norman troops came to Ireland on the instigation of the exiled Leinster king, Dermot mac Murrough, to help him regain the province; they continued their conquest and soon occupied a considerable territory for themselves. Gradually, the Anglo-Normans integrated, married into leading Gaelic families, and adopted the Gaelic language and traditions.[43] From the fourteenth century onwards, influential Anglo-Norman families combined the theme of the 'seal-woman' with the Gaelic perception of a mythical clan-ancestress, apparently to stress their legitimate right over the occupied territory.

Lucky Mermaids: Kilcooley Abbey, County Tipperary (left); **Clonfert, County Galway** (right)

The small number of Irish mermaid stones stem from areas where the lore of a mermaid descent was current. The carvings occur primarily on the internal walls of fifteenth century churches, and are usually interpreted in the Christian context as a warning against sin, though the link of the mermaid to several influential families would rather suggest that the carvings were meant to represent the ancestress of a founder or benefactor of the respective building. In modern times, her protective and tutelary aspect has been re-discovered, when visitors touch and rub the carving as talismans. Several little mermaids have become smooth and shiny from the reverence thus received.

The Children of the Mermaid, Enniscrone, County Sligo

The local chieftain Thady O'Dowd, so the story goes, had once spotted a beautiful mermaid sleeping on the shore. He took her cloak and hid it, thereby removing her ability to return to the sea. O'Dowd and the mermaid married and had seven children. One day, the youngest saw the father moving the cloak to another hiding place. The child told his mother, who immediately recovered the cloak and went off towards the shore. The children pleaded with her to stay, but the call from the sea was too strong. The mermaid turned six of her children into stones, forming a small stone circle overlooking the bay, and took the youngest with her when she disappeared into the waters. Until recently it was believed that the petrified children of the mermaid would bleed whenever a member of the O'Dowd family is about to die. Since the stone circle lies on private land and not accessible, the legend became recently attached to a set of stones that appear from the sea at low tide.[44]

Particularly in the coastal regions in the west of the country, popular tradition tended to apply the theme of a water-borne ancestress to the mermaid. Several Irish and Anglo-Norman families claimed a mermaid as their ancestress, and attributed her with all the ancient traits of a goddess guarding over her descendants as a tutelary spirit. Tales of mortal men marrying mermaids featured prominently in oral lore.

Witch Stones

In 1233, Pope Gregory IX issued the first papal bull to encourage the persecution of people who deviated from the dogma issued by Rome. Soon, alleged witches – and to a lesser extent sorcerers – were to bear the brunt of the inquisition, the hunt for heretics and dissidents. Between 1484 and 1782, about 300,000 people were murdered in Europe for their alleged pact with the devil – the majority of them were women.

Wherever witch hysteria has raged, folklore will preserve the memory of witch stones and devil's rocks. Witch stones are usually said to mark the meeting places of witches or else the spot where an alleged witch had been murdered. The devil was traditionally believed to indicate his presence on earth by stamping the imprints of his feet into stones, or by leaving the impression of his bottom while he sat waiting for a victim to seduce. These concepts of witch and devil were alien to the Celtic Church, who had from her formative years accepted the knowledge and practice of magic and sorcery as valued attributes of saints. Hence, apart from the anglicised regions of Scotland, the European witchcraft hysteria had comparatively little impact in Celtic areas.[45]

Consequently, the witch in the inquisitorial sense does not hold a prominent place in Irish folklore, and the characteristics attributed to 'a witch' in popular lore would usually allow to identify her as a derivation of the Cailleach Bhéarra. Slightly different is the image of the witch in aetiological tales explaining the presence of conspicuous stones in the neighbourhood of round towers, but even here she does not necessarily appear as an opponent to Christianity, and her image is clearly distinct from the European perceptions of a witch.

Wood-Martin gives an illustration of her hostile attitude when he tells of how a witch cast spells at a saint to prevent him from completing his round tower. The saint leaped down and struck the woman with his hammer, thereby turning her into the stone that lies near the base of the edifice; nevertheless, the

**The Witch Stone,
Inis Cealtra, County Clare**

*The round tower of Inis
Cealtra on Lough Derg in
County Clare has never been
finished. Local folklore blames
an old witch, who had passed
by when work was in progress.
Since the woman was not
happy about the construction
of the tower, she refused to
say the expected benediction
on the work, that is 'God bless
the work' or 'Bail ó Dhia ar an
obair'. The mason was deeply
annoyed. By a blow of his
hammer, he metamorphosed
the witch into a stone – the
boulder which was later
adorned with a High Cross –
and never resumed the work
on the building.*[46]

witch was successful, as the tower remained unfinished. Wood-Martin does not give the name of the saint nor locate the round tower, but the story seems to be a variant of the lore concerning the round tower on Inis Cealtra in County Clare.[47]

Elsewhere, the Cailleach or witch appears herself as the builder of round towers. The construction of the round tower at Meelick in County Mayo is popularly attributed to the Cailleach Bhéarra and her intention to erect a monument that would reach to the sky. She abandoned her plan only when a boy had passed and mocked her. Enraged, she jumped from the unfinished edifice, leaving the impressions of her knees in a stone at its base.[48]

The Witch Stone, Antrim, County Antrim

Monastic life in Antrim began around 500 AD; the round tower dates from the tenth or eleventh century. Close to the tower lies a bullaun stone, a large boulder with two depressions. One of these hollows would always contain some water, and local history remembers that during the great draught in 1887 the gardener often used to drain the hollow, only to find it full of water the next morning. Folklore assigns the hollows to a witch or hag, who had built the tower, and jumped from the top when the structure was complete. She stumbled when landing on the stone, leaving the imprints of one knee and one elbow.[49]

Heroes, Kings and Giants

I shall turn inland to Callan mountain, near the top of which lies a very large stone, with a long 'Ogham' inscription, supposed to be the tomb of a heathen prince.[1]

Mary John Knott, *Two Months at Kilkee* (1836)

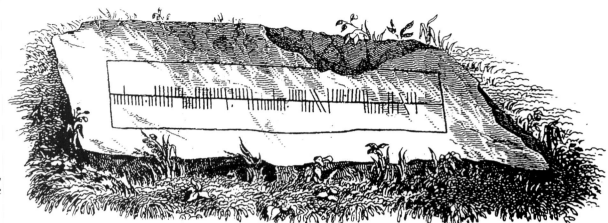

Conán's Grave,
Slieve Callan, County Clare

In Ireland the establishment of a patriarchal culture, which valued the ideals of aristocracy, heroic kings and warriors, began when Indo-European peoples filtered into the country during the Bronze Age. Ireland had large ore resources, especially of copper and gold. From about 2,500 BC, when the concept of metalworking was introduced and metal gradually replaced stone as the major raw material, the country entered the Bronze Age, which might have lasted until about 700 BC.[2]

The significant cultural change is obvious in the separation of burial places from ritual sites from the end of the Stone Age. Tombs and graves became simpler and smaller – the old tradition found its last expression in the construction of the so-called wedge tombs of the early Bronze Age. Finds of highly accomplished personal ornaments, of elaborate gold and bronze artefacts and of sophisticated weapons, buried with the dead or deposited in sacrificial hoards, give material evidence of the formation of an increasingly violent aristocratic society. Communities became more structured and would have consisted of farmers, craftspeople and warriors, with the different tribes led by aristocratic territorial chieftains. A rather formal religion emerged, no longer focusing on the earth goddess but cherishing a pantheon of male and female deities.[3]

Ritual activities to please the divine shifted outdoors, and were presumably performed at the new types of stone monuments that appeared with the Bronze Age: elaborately decorated natural rocks, and upright pillar stones, standing on their own or arranged in circles and rows. Bronze Age monuments are

Clochabhile, Lough Gur, County Limerick

Clochabhile or the Stone of the Sacred Tree unites in itself the Celtic concepts of sacred trees and central stones. The pillar stands a short distance from the Grange Stone Circle at Lough Gur, an area traditionally linked to the goddess Áine and to Fer Í, Eogabal and Eoghan, the mythical ancestors of the mighty Eóganacht sept. The current use of the term eo, which is Irish for 'a yew', illustrates the high reverence of the clan for that species of tree and we can easily imagine that Clochabhile was formerly joined by a yew considered sacred to the Eóganachta. The tree and its history are lost, but local lore knows of a magic tree on the bottom of Lough Gur, which would only surface once in seven years.[4]

frequently aligned with the sunrise or sunset on summer or winter solstice, or on spring or autumn equinox. While such orientations testify to the continuation of solar worship during the Bronze Age, we have no certainty of the nature of the ceremonies carried out at these sites.

The first groups of Celtic peoples might have appeared in Ireland during the last five or six centuries BC. Their arrival coincides roughly with the dawn of the Iron Age, which ended in the fifth century AD with the introduction of Christianity. Themselves a branch of Indo-European warrior tribes who had dominated Central Europe, the Celts shared the heroic, aristocratic ideal and the polytheistic religious concept of their Bronze Age precursors. Their communities were based on clans, ruled by local chieftains and provincial priest-kings, and their religion endorsed the cult of several female and male deities.

Whether it was out of respect for older sacred values or for a shared belief in the underlying symbolism, the Celts did not destroy earlier ritual sites and monuments; instead, they used them for their own assemblies and ceremonies. We can assume that they also took over parts of the practices that were initially linked to those sites, and incorporated them into their own rites and traditions; the memory of Celtic ceremonies at earlier sites has perhaps influenced their popular designations as druidic places of worship. In early Celtic Ireland, there would have been no religious buildings, and no images of deities. In agreement with their worship of nature, the Celts would have venerated the presence of goddesses and gods in sacred features of the landscape. Wells and trees, mountains and unmodified stones and earlier stone monuments were taken for divine abodes, and ceremonial assemblies and festivals were established around them. A class of sacred stone which the Celts particularly valued was the central pillar, a monolith marking the centre or axis of a territory. Apart from a few dome-shaped pillars, decorated in the La Tène style of early continental Celts, the central stones were usually phallic stones or unmodified pillars.

As with the Neolithic inhabitants of Ireland, we have no written historical accounts of the Indo-European conquest of the Bronze and Iron Age, and the ancient myths provide the only source of information on that period of social, political and religious change.

We have already seen that the *Leabhar Gabhála* attributes the division of Ireland into provinces to the Fir Bolg; the same people are credited with the introduction of sacral kingship. The Tuatha Dé Danann introduced druidry and talismans; they established the cult of the Daghdha, a father god and the counterpart to the mother goddess Danu, and of other great warrior gods with their magic weapons: Lugh Lámhfhada who carried an invincible spear; Nuadhu with his sword from which no enemy could escape.

The Eglone, a petrified giant, Highwood, County Sligo

The Tuatha Dé Danann's contributions to the system of sacral kingship were the Lia Fáil, the miraculous stone to determine the legitimacy of a prospective king, and the idea of a land goddess as the wife of a reigning king.[5]

The motif of a warrior god as the lover of the land goddess features repeatedly in Indo-European myths, and stands possibly behind the pre-historic practice to erect pairs of pillar stones. Where one of the stones is tall, thin and sharp-topped, while the second appears rather small, square and blunt-topped, the pair is often taken for a representation of a divine couple, or of the female and male principles. Their initial function is uncertain, though it is easy to imagine that they were gateposts to sacred or secular enclosures. The local designation, 'Gates of Glory' for a pair of stones near Dingle in County Kerry, and the position of the pillars Blocc and Bluigne at the entrance to the sacred site on the Hill of Tara in County Meath support this notion.[6]

Medieval literature and popular tradition transformed the mythological warrior gods into great heroes, mythical kings, and – in exaggeration of their deeds or where the names were lost – into giants. Tales of kingship and battle, of competitions and contests of strengths, and of feats and deaths of mythical and historical champions were attached to monuments of the Bronze and Iron Ages, and reflect particularly early Celtic society. In Christian contexts echoes of the ancient gods survived in the lore of early saints and their struggle against several personifications of paganism.

Druid Circles and Giants Dance

Nineteenth-century antiquarians called them Druid Circles and – lacking modern archaeological dating methods – tended to attribute their construction to the Celts. Current surveys illustrate that the stone circles of Ireland definitely predate the arrival of the Celts and belong predominately to the Bronze Age. The circle at Newgrange, probably the oldest in Ireland, might even have been erected as part of a

The Beaghmore Stone Circles, County Tyrone

In 1945, turf cutting revealed the existence of a magnificent Bronze Age ceremonial site on Beaghmore. It was subsequently excavated in the 1940s, and re-examined in 1960. At present, seven stone circles, eight alignments and twelve cairns can be seen, but there are more monuments still hidden in the ground. The stones are characteristically small and are locally referred to as 'dragon teeth'.[7]

Drombeg Stone Circle, Rosscarberry, County Cork

The Drombeg Stone Circle or Druid's Altar is aligned with the sunset at winter solstice. It has a rather dark reputation, probably arising from the find of the cremated remains of an adolescent in its centre. In 1903, the antiquarian Franklin suggested the remains were evidence of human sacrifice, and compared them with the infant bones and sawn skeletons from stone circles in ancient Palestine. About 30 years later, Miss Geraldine Cummings, a psychic, came to survey the Drombeg circle; she visualised priests killing human offerings, a 'Great Day of Blood Sacrifice' towards the end of December and dances where men and women stabbed each other in frenzy. Subsequently, the Druid's Altar was regarded as cursed and 'guarded by the spirits of darkness'.[10]

Stone Age monument.[8] It is interesting to note that the ancient myths of Ireland agree largely with modern archaeology when they attribute the construction of the first stone circles in the country to a pre-Celtic race, the Tuatha Dé Danann. At the same time, the myths contain a justification for the term Druid Circles when they state that it was the Tuatha that introduced magic knowledge and druidism to the country.

Ireland has about 240 stone circles; significant concentrations occur in mid-Ulster and south west Munster; several smaller groups exist in the east and the west of the country.

In contrast to the circles elsewhere, those in mid-Ulster feature hardly in popular traditions, although they are not less impressive. But their builders used considerably smaller stones, and when the sites were deserted due to a catastrophic climate change during the Bronze Age, around 1,160 BC, the stone circles gradually disappeared under layers of blanket bog, and were only discovered in modern times.[9]

The circles of larger stones must have made an enormous impact on the incoming Celts, who should use the monuments to hold assemblies or to perform religious rituals. The names of several circles, as well as the popular traditions associated with them into fairly recent times, indicate particularly a link to ancient seasonal festivals. The Beltany Circle in County Donegal, for instance, recalls the celebration of Bealtaine which marked the beginning of summer on 1 May; the Grange Circle at Lough

Gur is aligned to the sun at both the harvest feast of Lughnasa at the beginning of August and the start of winter and the new year at Samhain.

Archaeologists have discovered cremated remains – apparently remnants of sacrifices – in many stone circles. Besides this, there is no reliable evidence on the ancient rituals and ceremonies carried out in and around stone circles in Celtic or earlier times. We have to look at folklore as the only possible source of information, and find that stone circles – in Ireland and abroad – are conspicuously often linked to the aspect of dancing. Dance has probably been the earliest expression of worship and celebration; the oldest material evidence of ritual dances in ancient Europe are Mesolithic rock decorations from the Mediterranean.

Writing in the twelfth century, Giraldus Cambrensis informs his readers about the origin and fate of the Giant's Dance, a splendid stone circle in the plain of Kildare. The stones, he relates, stem from Africa and were brought to Ireland by giants. Later, Merlin magically lifted them through the air to England, and reassembled them as the Stonehenge monument in the plain of Salisbury. In Irish popular tradition, the dancers at stone circles would usually be fairies; only from the seventeenth or the eighteenth century, when the keeping of the holy day began to be an issue for the established Churches, stone circles were occasionally interpreted as petrified dancers who had dared to enjoy themselves on a Sunday.[11]

Stone-Fingers and Fairy Rocks — Sacred Stones or Practical Devices?

Territorial markers, astrological observatories and ancient calendars or sacred symbols at ritual sites – the exact purpose of stone rows lies in the dark, unlikely to ever be revealed. Modern archaeology assigns the monuments to the Bronze Age and would use the term 'stone alignment' to denote rows with a clear orientation towards other megalithic monuments, conspicuous physical features in the landscape, or towards the sun or moon.

With regards to design and layout, two major groups have been identified: long rows of rather small stones, and shorter alignments consisting of up to six stones with an average height of 6 to 10

The Battle of Moytirra and the Stone Circles of Cong, County Mayo
(opposite page)

Around the Glebe Stone Circles just outside Cong, strange fairy dancers are said to appear from time to time. They are believed to be the spirits of the Tuatha Dé Danann celebrating their victory over the Fir Bolg in the first Battle of Moytirra. The Fir Bolg had engaged the Formorian champion Balor, whose evil eye was feared for its power to evaporate his enemies. The Tuatha Dé Danann, well aware of the peril, erected stone circles and painted the images of warriors on them to deceive Balor. As expected, his eye failed to destroy the stones. Balor, convinced that his evil eye had lost its destructive energy, left the battlefield – and without his assistance the Fir Bolg were soon defeated.[12]

feet.[13] Seen from a distance, particularly the latter group can appear like massive fingers reaching out from the ground; accordingly several stone alignments are popularly known as finger stones or giant fingers.

The interpretation of stone rows as *Fear Breagha* or sham men is a popular motif in the lore of saints from the early Celtic Church, who would often have emphasised the might of the new religion by petrifying sinners or druids and other opponents of the Christian doctrine. In the context of myths and hero tales, *Fear Breagha* appear occasionally as sham warriors, erected to deceive hostile armies. Local tradition regarding *Na Fir Bréige* on Cape Clear in County Cork illustrates that this idea persisted into fairly modern times. Overlooking the south-western point of the island, the stone alignment on Sliabh Ard is among the most impressive ancient monuments on Cape Clear. Island lore relates that the stones were only erected in this prominent position after a French fleet had landed to Bantry Bay

Fionn mac Cumhaill's Fingers, Castletara, County Cavan

They are locally referred to as finger stones or Fionn mac Cumhaill's Fingers, though the story of how the hero's fingers came to be on Shantemon Hill is no longer remembered. The stone align-ment dates to the Bronze Age; when Celtic tribes settled in the area they acknowledged the sanctity of the site, and installed the chieftains of the influential O'Reilly clan in the shadow of the finger stones. Until the first decades of the twentieth century, young people gathered on the hill for the 'Pattern of Shantemon' on Bilberry Sunday in August, probably a remnant of the ancient harvest festival of Lughnasa.[14]

The Clonfinlough Stone, County Offaly

In the 1930s the Clonfinlough Stone was popularly called the Fairy Stone or the Piper's Rock, and stories were current of mysterious horsemen circling the stone to the music of fairy pipers, who left their imprints in the stone. The Clonfinlough Stone was first described in 1895. Since then, a natural origin had been assigned to some of the motifs on its surface, including the footprints. Others are artificial, and one can assume that the stone had once been of spiritual significance.[19]

in 1796. The pillars were clad in uniforms and 'armed' with wooden sticks to give the impression of soldiers, to discourage any hostile forces from approaching Cape Clear.[15]

The initial purpose of rock art, that is – carvings on standing stones or on the exposed surface of the grown rock – is as obscure as the original function of stone alignments.[16] About 80 exemplars of rock art have been recorded to date, predominately in the south west and the north west of the country. The motifs – cup-marks and circles, spirals and dots – show some similarities to the designs used in Irish passage grave art, but rock art is certainly a distinctive group in its own right.[17]

Experts have offered a variety of theories on the function of these decorated boulders; a recurrent one is their interpretation as the earliest types of practical maps. Twentieth-century surveys in Britain showed that a very high percentage of decorated stones were discovered in the vicinity of gold or copper deposits; they might therefore have been magical symbols or practical maps of early metal diggers.[18]

Comparable studies from Ireland are not published, but considerable Bronze Age copper finds are record-ed from the south west, where the most impressive examples of Irish rock art have been discovered.

Popularly, decorated Bronze Age boulders are often linked with the fairies. The cup-marks are said to be imprints left by the little folk sitting or dancing on the stone, and into the twentieth-century offerings of flowers and fruit were on occasion deposited to please them. Cup-marks on standing stones are some-times taken for the fingerprints of giants, while impressions in the shape of feet would primarily be associated with mythical ancestors and inaugural ceremonies of Gaelic chieftains. We will also meet decorated Bronze Age stones in the context of Christian stone lore, since early Irish saints have apparently felt the need to reinterpret or eradicate an earlier cult at several boulders.[20]

Monoliths and the Myth of the Heroic Warrior

Monoliths or individual upright stone pillars are a familiar feature all over the country, with some 600 examples being identified so far. They appear in various forms and shapes, and we must consider that they might belong to different periods from the Neolithic or Bronze Age to the medieval period, and were certainly erected for a wide range of purposes. The most common term for a monolith is standing stone or pillar stone, or in Irish *gallán*, *dallán*, and *liágan*; monoliths associated with kingship and terri-torial power, with battle and warfare would often bear specific names.[21]

In ancient heroic contexts, pillar stones feature recurrently as memorials to individual historical or pseudo-historical characters, and to their battles and heroic feats. These stones are often named after the respective hero, or play a significant role in the popular traditions of a momentous event. Thought to preserve the spirit or essence of the heroes, memorial stones were considered sacred and survived into our days. Especially during the nineteenth century, several commemorative pillars were misinterpreted as grave markers, but excavations did not reveal any traces of burial.

The continuity of the desire to preserve the memory of great martial heroes in stone is evident in the large number of massive boulders or standing stones bearing commemorative plaques to the battles of 1798, or to the fighters of 1916. In contrast to earlier memorials, however, these stones are inter-changeable and did not attract popular traditions.[22]

The first Battle of Moytirra and the Lia Lugha

Medieval texts dealing with the first Battle of Moytirra relate that the Tuatha Dé Danann, led by king Nuadhu, beat the Fir Bolg and took the kingship of Ireland from them. Nuadhu, however, had lost his arm in the fight. Since a bodily blemish was unacceptable in a king, he had to resign from his position until his severed limb was restored by the magic healer, Dian Céacht. Nuadhu fell in the second Battle of Moytirra against the Formorians, but the Tuatha Dé Danann, with their hero Lugh Lámhfhada, were victorious in the end. Lugh is the young warrior god who gave his name to the festival of Lughnasa; his epithet means long-armed and is a reference to his generosity and his skill in battle.

The Mayo village of Neale, a few miles from Cong, is traditionally identified as the site of the first Battle of Moytirra against the Fir Bolg. Local folklore – obviously temped by the epithet of Lugh – has combined the memory of this battle with elements from the myths of the second Battle of Moytirra. Current narratives relate that Lugh Lámhfhada was the unfortunate hero who had lost his arm in the fighting, or else that he was slain on the battlefield.

Lia Lugha or the Long Stone, Neale, County Mayo

The Lia Lugha at the entrance to the village of Neale is alternatively pointed out as a marker of the spot of the Lugh Lámhfhada's death or as the place where his severed arm lies buried.[23]

The death of Cúchulainn and the Big Man's Stone

Cúchulainn was the son of the Tuatha Dé Danann leader Lugh Lámhfhada, and the champion of the Red Branch Knights or *Craeb Ruad*, the heroes from the Ulster Cycle of tales. They stood in the service of King Conchobhar mac Nessa who ruled the province of Ulster from his residence at Eamhain Mhacha, today known as Navan Fort. The earliest texts concerning Cúchulainn survived from the ninth or eleventh century, but they have certainly derived from older narratives.[24]

The tales stress his extraordinary bravery and skills on the battlefield. He is the celebrated hero of the *Táin Bó Cuailnge* and the ensuing fight against the armies of the Connacht Queen Meadhbh. Cúchulainn died, overcome by treachery and magic near the village of Knockbridge in the Cooley area of County Louth.

The Big Man's Stone, Knockbridge, County Louth

Sorcery had weakened Cúchulainn, so the champion slept for three nights and three days in the village of Knockbridge to recover. He returned to the battlefield, but a specially crafted spear hit him so hard that his intestines fell out. Fatally wounded, Cúchulainn strapped himself to a pillar stone - hence known as the Big Man's Stone – so that he would die standing on his feet and facing the enemy. When he died at last, Cúchulainn released a deep sigh of agony, causing the pillar to crack. For three days, his opponents did not dare to approach him; only when a bird descended on his shoulder did they trust that he was dead. They cut the veins of his hand to take his sword and they severed his head as a trophy.[25]

The Red Pillar and the last pagan king of Ireland

The area of Cruachain near Tulsk in County Roscommon has been an extensive cemetery for Bronze Age warriors. The Celts acknowledged the sacred status of the site and linked it to their own war goddess, the *Mór-Ríoghain* or Morrigan. From about 300 BC, Cruachain became one of the major centres of Celtic Ireland; Rathcroghan was both assembly site and royal residence, and at nearby Carnfree, the kings of Connacht were inaugurated.[26]

Dáithí's Stone, or the Red Pillar, Tulsk, County Roscommon

On a hillock near Rathcroghan stands *An Coirthe Dearg*, the Red Pillar. The sandstone pillar is more popularly dubbed Dáithí's Stone, and tradition holds that it was erected to mark the grave of Dáithí or Nath Í, an historical king who died in about 445 AD. Dáithí was the last pagan king of Ireland and a fierce opponent of the new religion. He allegedly destroyed the tower of a Christian king at the foot of Sliabh n-Ealpa, believed to be the Alps, but more likely a mistranslation of the old name Alba for Scotland. When his victim prayed to God for revenge, a flash of lightning struck Dáithí and killed him instantly. His corpse was returned to Ireland to be interred under the Red Pillar.[27]

Cloch-a-Phoil and the Escape of Eochaidh of Leinster

Local lore links the large holed flagstone to the historical fourth- or fifth-century king Niall of the Nine Hostages (*Niall Naoi Ghiallach*) and his opponent Eochaidh, son of the Leinster king Eanna Cinsealach. Writing in the seventeenth century, the historian Keating renders a very detailed account of the story; less elaborate versions are still current in the Aghade area.

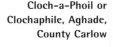
Cloch-a-Phoil or Clochaphile, Aghade, County Carlow

Eochaidh, so Keating, was refused entertainment in the house of Niall's chief poet, and in a fit of rage, he burnt the poet's house and killed his only son. In retaliation, Niall invaded the province of Leinster. The poet pitied the sufferings of the innocent people, and he persuaded Niall to offer peace under the condition that Eochaidh be handed over to him for punishment. The people of Leinster agreed and Eochaidh was chained to the pillar stone. When the poet sent nine archers to shoot his victim, Eochaidh broke the iron chain, killed some of the archers and fled from Ireland. Niall exiled him but the two counterparts met in battle abroad. Eochaidh killed Niall, and returned to Ireland to gain possession of Leinster and to rule the province for many years to come.[28]

The Clochaphile was once renowned for its healing virtues, and up to the eighteenth century infants were passed through the hole to cure or prevent 'rickets'.

Viking memorial stones and the death of Prince Aralt

From the poetical Edda we learn that the Vikings, too, erected memorial stones to their dead. In Ireland, material evidence for this practice survived at Castledermot in County Kildare, and near Dunlavin in County Wicklow. The Dunlavin area is traditionally associated with the year 998 or 999 and the Battle of Gleann Máma between Brian Boru's troops and the army of Sitric, the Danish king of Dublin.[29]

In the townland of Cryhelp just outside the village of Dunlavin stands a granite pillar with an unusual rectangular hole. In 1931, the antiquarian Walshe has published a survey of the area and refers to the local belief that the pillar marked the spot of the death and burial of the Danish prince, Aralt.

The Grave of Prince Aralt, Dunlavin, County Wicklow (left) **and Viking grave marker, Castledermot, County Kildare**

He was, according to the Annals of the Four Masters, the brother of King Sitric and next in line to the Dublin throne. Today, only a very faint memory survives of a Viking burial in the area. Entirely lost are recollections of marriage celebrations at the stone, which were also mentioned in Walshe's account. Merely a locally held reluctance to put an arm through the opening for fear of evil consequences, however, indicates a former ceremonial significance to the pillar.[30]

The only Scandinavian 'hog-back' memorial stone or grave marker found so far in Ireland is preserved in the old graveyard of Castledermot in County Kildare. The zig-zag motif on the reverse occurs frequently on picture stones from Gotland; the island off the Swedish east coast has been an important Viking trading post.

Patrick Sarsfield and the Treaty Stone of Limerick

Cromwell's conquest of Ireland and the ensuing wars left Catholic Ireland devastated. New hope arose when James II, himself of the Catholic faith, became king of England. Consequently, James II found support in Ireland, when English Protestants called for William of Orange to expel James' from the throne. Following James' defeat in the Battle of the Boyne in 1690, and his flight to France, William expected James' Irish supporters to surrender. It was Patrick Sarsfield who vigorously opposed a capitulation, and the war continued, culminating in the siege of Limerick

The Treaty Stone, Limerick city

In spite of historical accounts and contemporary witnesses who maintain that the Treaty of Limerick had been signed on a table, folk memory insists that Sarsfield and Ginkel signed the Articles on the Treaty Stone. The boulder was brought from the site of the Williamite camp into Limerick, and in 1865 Rickard Tinsley, then mayor of Limerick, initiated the erection of a pedestal for the Treaty Stone near Thomond Bridge, where the decisive battle of 1691 has been fought.[31]

in 1691. After suffering great casualties, Patrick Sarsfield eventually approached William's general, Ginkel, to negotiate the terms for a capitulation. On 3 October 1691, they reached an agreement and signed the 'Articles of Limerick', commonly know as the Treaty of Limerick. Influential Protestants opposed the 'civil articles' of the agreement, which dealt basically with the rights of Catholics to exercise their religion, with the restoration of confiscated land and with pardon for war incidents. The Protestant Parliament delayed the implementation of the Treaty, and instead put down a comprehensive body of suppressive laws, commonly known as Penal Laws, which restricted the rights of the Catholic population of Ireland even further. In 1697, when the Articles of Limerick were finally to be ratified, the Penal Laws prevented their full implementation, and the agreement of 1691 was practically void.[32]

Fionn mac Cumhaill's Stone-Throwing Contests

The most popular character with regards to the folklore of stones is Fionn mac Cumhaill; throughout the country, we find his name so frequently linked to ancient stone monuments and topographical features, that he – like the Cailleach Bhéarra – truly deserves the title 'shaper of the Irish landscape'.[33]

Among scholars it is not undisputed whether Fionn mac Cumhaill was a historical character who lived in the third century AD, or a fictional hero from early medieval romances. Texts relating to Fionn were written down from the eighth century and constitute the Fenian Cycle of tales, a body of narratives dealing with Fionn and his warrior band, the Fianna, who stood in the service of King Cormac mac Airt. The tales seem to have their roots in older traditions, and Fionn's personality reflects in many ways the archaic seer Find, who in turn seems to be an emanation of the Celtic or Indo-European god, Vindos.[34] One of the major themes of the literary Fenian tradition is the feud between Fionn's Leinster Fianna and the Connacht Fianna under the leadership of Goll mac Morna. Although bonded by marriage connections, the old animosities between Fionn and Goll never ceased, and resulted in numerous battles between the heroes. Folklore has readily adapted the theme, and transformed the fights into contests of strength between Fionn and his rivals. Since popular tradition has exaggerated the extraordinary virtue and strength of the literary characters, folklore would characteristically portray Fionn and his opponents as giants. The recurrent description of Fionn's counterpart as a Scottish or English giant is certainly a reflection of the literary tradition of Goll's temporary banishment to Scotland.

Extremely prominent was the motif of Fionn's contests in the form of stone-throwing competitions. Occasionally, such competitions are ascribed to anonymous giants, though the derivation of these tales from the Fionn tradition is apparent. In County Laois, for instance, it is told that the giant from Clopock had once challenged his counterpart from Dunamase. The latter did not manage to throw his stone further than from Dunamase to Castledermot, County Kildare; on seeing what he regarded a poor performance, the Clopock giant laughed so hard that he dropped his own pillar; it sank partly into the ground, where it remains to this day.[35]

Throughout the country, storytellers made use of the theme where the origin of conspicuous standing stones, of curious natural rocks or of erratic boulders on hills or mountain tops, demanded an explanation.

Fionn's Split Rock, Easky, County Sligo (right)

The origin of the conspicuous Ice Age erratic is attributed to Fionn, who challenged a comrade to throw a stone from Ox Mountain into the sea. His comrade succeeded, but Fionn's stone fell short. In anger, he split the rock with his sword. Tradition has it that it is possible to walk through the gap twice but it would close on you on your third try.[36]

Cloghmore, Rostrevor, County Down (opposite page)

A popular narrative dealing with the contest between Fionn mac Cumhaill and an English giant claims that the Isle of Man was, in fact, a sod taken by Fionn from the site of Lough Neagh and flung at his adversary. In the course of the same contest, as maintained in County Down, Fionn had attempted to throw a huge rock – the Cloghmore, an erratic boulder of estimated 40 tons weight – at his opponent. Luckily for Fionn's rival, the device fell short and landed on Rostrevor Mountain.

**The Long Stone,
Punchestown, County Kildare**

*Standing about 23 feet high,
the granite pillar near the
racecourse at Punchestown is
the tallest monolith in Ireland.
It is a characteristic 'long
stone' from the Bronze Age,
distinguished by its height, its
slightly pointed slender
appearance and the evidence
of human burial at its base.
Tradition holds that Fionn
mac Cumhaill hurled the
'long stone' and several
similar pillars in the area
from his headquarters on
the Hill of Allen.[37]*

   With archaeology and geology not yet developed, it was beyond imagination that anyone but giants or heroes of extraordinary strength had ever been able to move and handle such massive boulders. If the respective stones show small indentations, folklore attributed them eagerly to the mighty grip of a hero and took their presence to underline the veracity of the tale.[38]

   Pillars bearing the imprints of their fingers belong especially to the northern half, and we encounter them from Fionn's Fingerprint on a dolmen at Goward in County Down to the Giant's Finger Stone, a cup-marked Bronze Age pillar at Bellanascaddan in County Donegal. Several of such finger stones are believed to preserve the essence of the hero's vigour and courage, and to pass a bit of these qualities to those who place their fingers in the indentations. A powerful example for a strength-releasing finger stone stands on the western slope of Slieve Anierin in County Leitrim, cast by Fionn mac Cumhaill to its location from the far side of Lough Allen.[39]

   The Mottee Stone, also known as Fionn mac Cumhaill's hurling stone, has a different miraculous potential. The massive granite boulder sits on top of Croaghanmore in the Wicklow Mountains and would, according to local lore, leave its position once a year on the eve of Mayday to walk down and take a drink at the 'Meetings of the Water' near Avoca. The lore of stones that would move

Six Fingers, Williamstown, County Carlow

The grooved pillar stone near Rathvilly is another device of Fionn, this time supposed to be cast from Eagle's Hill. The origin of the six grooves, or 'six fingers', is uncertain; in Ireland, as in Brittany and Germany, where similar pillars occur, they have long been considered artificially modified Iron Age monuments; currently scholars prefer to assign a natural origin by erosion to the grooves.[40]

about and go for a drink at particular times of the year is extremely scarce in Ireland; the motif has apparently been introduced from abroad, presumably from Wales or the south of England, where it is quite popular and usually attached to pre-historic standing stones.[41]

The Legacy of Irish Giants

We have already seen that folklore would frequently assign the origin of standing stones and conspicuous natural boulders to Fionn mac Cumhaill or alternatively to an anonymous giant. The same link appears in the lore of Neolithic dolmens or Bronze Age wedge cairns in areas where those monuments are not explicitly connected to tales of Diarmaid and Gráinne or the Cailleach Bhéarra. The association to other-world women or to the complex of Fenian tales, however, remains intact, though sometimes very vague and not immediately noticeable. Obvious is the link in the Ox Mountain area of County Sligo, where several dolmens and wedge cairns are alternatively pointed out as the Giant's Griddle Stones or the Griddles of the Fianna. In the lore of the Lickerstown dolmen or Céadach's Grave in County Kilkenny, the Fenian tradition is less apparent. The story tells of the giants Céadach and Goll, who had a fierce argument concerning Goll's daughter Grania. In the ensuing fight, Goll slays Céadach. The dying hero fell and left an indentation on a boulder, which was then assembled with additional pillars to build him a fitting tomb.[42] Though Fionn mac Cumhaill is not mentioned in the tale, the characters come never-theless from the literary Fenian tradition: Grania is Gráinne who had eloped with Diarmaid; the giant Goll is Fionn's opponent Goll mac Morna, and Céadach is a foreign prince who was attracted by the fame of the Fianna and came to Ireland to join the warrior band.

Where hilltop cairns are explained as the graves of heroes or giants, we can also expect to find at least a shadowy presence of a female character. Since such cairns would primarily be considered the sacred abodes of the earth goddess or her later manifestations, only their lovers, husbands or sons would be able to gain access to the chambers inside the cairns.

Medieval texts have the Daghdha, lover of the goddess Bóinn, and their son Aonghus, reside in the cairns at Brú na Bóinne; Fraoch, the son of Bóinn's sister Bé Find is buried at Carnfree (Carn Fraoich) near Tulsk in County Roscommon; and the Tuatha Dé Danann king, Bodhbh, rests in the

Browne's Hill Dolmen, County Carlow
(opposite page)

The massive granite capstone of the dolmen is, with an estimated weight of 100 tons, amongst the heaviest of its kind in Europe. Antiquarians dubbed the dolmen 'Pagan Altar', but local lore attributes its origin to the joint works of a giant and a poor woman. The giant, once walking the country, happened to stumble over a massive stone; he picked it up and angrily threw it out of his way. The boulder landed on Browne's Hill near Carlow town, and lay unnoticed until a poor woman and her children passed by on a stormy night. In her desperation, the woman lifted the stone and propped it up, so they had shelter for the night.[43]

Prince Connell's Grave, Corracloona, County Leitrim

Feart Chonaill Flaith or Prince Connell's Grave is the official name of the ruined court cairn near Kilticlogher in the north east of County Leitrim. In the locality, the identity of the prince is not remembered, and neither is his burial in the tomb referred to in any of the older folklore accounts from the district. The link of the monument to the prince derives obviously from a supposition of antiquarians, who might have thought of Connall Gulban, son of Niall of the Nine Hostages and founder of the kingdom of Tír Chonaill (Donegal). The historical Connall met his death when he chased raiders down to south County Leitrim, and was buried there in the Fenagh area.[44]

cairn on Slievenamon, County Tipperary. According to Armagh folklore, Fionn mac Cumhaill lies buried in the southern cairn on Slieve Gullion, which is also known as the 'house' of his lover, the Cailleach Bhéarra. From their union sprang a son, Oísín, who was himself buried under a cairn near Downpatrick in County Down.[45]

By Lough Gill in County Sligo, two cairns on neighbouring hilltops are linked with the giant warriors Oghamra and Romera. A romantic tale, explaining the origin of Lough Gill, relates that Oghamra fell in love with Romera's daughter Gile or Gealla; when her father found the couple together, he swore revenge. In the ensuing fight both men fell and a cairn was erected over each of them. The tears of the desperate girl were to form a lake which would take her name, Lough Gill. Back in about 1900, the same tale has been loosely connected with the Fianna, when Gile's father was described as a giant called Goll.[46]

Occasionally, the assumption of a giant hero's burial arose from the attempts of nineteenth-century antiquarians and historians to link the monuments to important characters from Ireland's unrecorded past. The lore of the burial of Conán Maol, the mischievous brother of Fionn's opponent Goll under the Ogham-inscribed pillar on Slieve Callan in County Clare is generally regarded as a fabrication of early antiquarians; nineteenth-century suggestions to take the Hag's Cairn at Loughcrew for the grave of the legendary law-giver Ollamh Fodhla has also been dismissed by modern scholars.

The recurrent close relation of Fionn mac Cumhaill with the lore of giants, especially in connection with Neolithic and Bronze Age structures, could easily lead to the presumption that Fionn is the only archetype of the giants of Irish popular tradition. But there has certainly been another ancient model for the image of the Irish giant – the mythical people of the Formorians. Myths depict them as one of the earliest inhabitants of Ireland; in the *Leabhar Gabhála* they make their first appearance when they destroyed Neimheadh's people and forced his sons to flee the country. Medieval texts are vague on the origin of the Formorians, and though usually cast as cruel raiding invaders who ventured into Ireland from across the sea, they might well have been the indigenous population living at the north-western fringes of the country. In myths and folklore, the Formorians are giants, and their memory survived particularly in the northern half of the country.

The Formorian champion was the one-eyed Balor, who supported the Fir Bolg in the first Battle of Moytirra at Cong, County Mayo, but retreated when being successfully deceived by the Tuatha Dé Danann and their sham warriors. In the second Battle of Moytirra, popularly set in the Lough Arrow region of County Sligo, Balor led his own people against the Tuatha Dé Danann.

**Giant's Causeway,
County Antrim**

*Clochan na bhFormharach
or Stones of the Formorians
was the old name for the
basalt columns, formed about
60 million years ago by molten
lava which cooled and shrunk
into about 40,000 hexagonal
pillars. They seem to disappear
under the sea and to resurface
again at the shore of the
Scottish island of Staffa,
giving rise to the tale that
they were built by the giant
Fionn mac Cumhaill, so he
could visit his equally gigantic
Scottish girlfriend.*[47]

The cairn at Heapstown in the Lough Arrow area of County Sligo was once popularly known as
'*Fás aon oíche*', the growth or work of one night. Some said that the name would derive from the
Cailleach who had the cairn built overnight; others attribute the monument to the Formorians. The
place would have been the site of the magic healing well of the physician, Dian Céacht, who used its
water to restore to health the Tuatha Dé Danann warriors who were wounded in the Battle of Moytirra.
When the Formorians realised the significance of the well, they came one night and buried the well
under a massive heap of stones.[48] The second Battle of Moytirra was a fight between the magic powers

The Eglone, Moytirra, County Sligo

The Eglone and several other impressive erratic boulders stand on high ground above Lough Arrow, a region which is popularly identified with the second Battle of Moytirra. Curiously, they do not directly feature in the tales of the fight between the Tuatha Dé Danann and the Formorians. Instead, local lore would attribute the origin of the Eglone, the massive square limestone boulder of nearly 18 feet height, to a magician, who had an argument with a giant. When the giant attempted to kill his opponent, the sorcerer petrified him by a stroke with his magic wand.[49]

of the Tuatha Dé Danann, and the physical force of the Formorians; it was eventually won by the Tuatha after Balor fell at the hands of his own grandson, Lugh Lámhfhada, thus fulfilling an ancient prophecy.

In oral tradition, the motif of a fight between vigour and sorcery would often appear as the story of a giant contesting a magician. Usually these tales end with the giants being metamorphosed into stone by the druidic art of their opponents. The origin of the Druid's Circle near Killarney, for instance, is attributed to a local magician who got tired of fighting two giants and their seven sons and turned them into stones.[50]

We have no written historical evidence of the Formorian invasions, but the tradition of their raids and cruelty must already have been embedded in Irish folklore by the end of the eighth century, when the Viking raiders began to appear at the west coast of Ireland.[51] The Vikings soon established permanent settlements along the coast, introduced an organised trading system, sophisticated seafaring technologies and the first coinage. We can assume a certain degree of social and cultural interchange between the native population and Viking settlers, but the image of the Norsemen in Irish folklore is essentially negative, and apparently modelled on the earlier perceptions of the raiding Formorians. Remembered as Lochlannaigh or Danes, folklore would generally portray Vikings as cruel and savage heathens; particularly in the lore of ancient stone monuments in the north of Ireland, the Danes are usually described as giants. The Mave Stone, the King's Fort and the Giant's Grave in the townland of Kilholye in County Derry are just a few examples of ancient structures attributed to Danish giants.

Saints, Sinners
and Stone Slabs of Heaven

'Ná sáruigther Seinglenn aitreb na lec nime' – *Let not the Old Glen be violated, the site of the stone slabs of heaven'*

attributed to St Colmcille (sixth century)

St Attracta's Well,
Monasteraden,
County Sligo

Although the introduction of Christianity to Ireland is commonly attributed to St Patrick, hagiographical texts and popular lore hold the tradition of pre-Patrician missionaries in the south and indicate that St Ailbhe of Emly, County Tipperary, St Ibar of Beg Ére, County Wexford, St Declan of Ardmore, County Waterford and St Ciarán of Saighir, County Offaly were in fact the first to preach the new religion in Ireland. In the south east of the country, it is firmly believed that as early as 402 AD, St Ciarán had celebrated the first Mass ever on Irish soil on Cape Clear in County Cork. Popular tradition is supported here by the saint's biography and by an entry in the Annals of Inisfallen, which claim that Ciarán heard about the new religious idea, and set out for Rome to learn more about it. In Rome he met St Declan and they both returned to Ireland in 402 to spread the Christian faith.

It is very likely that the new religious concept reached Ireland from the south through contacts with the Roman world, probably from as early as the fourth century. At about that time traders from North Africa settled in the south west of Ireland. Copts – early Christians from Egypt – fled their country

Gallán Chiaráin, Cape Clear, County Cork
(above), **pillar at Kilkieran,
County Kilkenny** (left)

*Cape Clear is closely associated with St Ciarán,
and island lore accredits the saint himself with
the erection of Gallán Chiaráin.*

*The pillar stands at Trá Chiaráin, and is still highly
revered by the islanders. Strangers were not
always aware of its sanctity, and the story goes
that once, a foreign fisherman sheltering
on the island during a storm tied his boat to the
pillar. That night Gallán Chiaráin bent its head,
so the rope slipped away and the boat was found
wrecked in the morning. The pillar has bent on
several similar occasions; one time, it even let go
of a rope that held a bull, and the animal took to
the sea and was drowned.*[1]

*The presence of a comparable but undecorated
stone at the saint's foundation of Kilkieran in
County Kilkenny suggests that Ciarán either
followed the ancient tradition of marking a
significant site with a phallic central stone, or
else that the saint has taken over sites of earlier
religious significance with their ritual stones,
and Christianised them by building an oratory
nearby, or by incising crosses into the pillar.*

and came to live on the islands off the Irish west coast. By 431 AD, the number of early Christian communities in Ireland was apparently substantial enough for Pope Celestine to send bishop Palladius to 'the Irish who believe in Christ'.[2]

Patrick started his missionary work in 432. His biographers claim that the saint had the whole island of Ireland Christianised when he died in 463 but it seems very unlikely that one person had actually completed the conversion of an entire country within such a short period of time. Nevertheless, it was Patrick who brought a significant overall change when he, unlike his predecessors, separated religious and political powers, which were formerly in the hands of pagan priest kings. Following their conversion, the kings retained their full political supremacy, as well as their palaces and inauguration

St Patrick's Grave, Downpatrick, County Down

Popular belief holds it that 'three saints do rest upon this hill: St Patrick, St Brigid, and St Colmcill'. The grave slab, which marks their alleged burial place, is of rather recent origin. In the nineteenth century, F.J. Pigger, then editor of the Ulster Journal of Archaeology, suggested that a granite boulder from the Mourne Mountains be brought to Downpatrick to honour the traditions of the burials.[3]

sites. Their religious authority, however, was transferred to the Church and executed by bishops.

Patrick's concept of a strictly structured Church, based on the Roman administrative principles of bishoprics, was not long lived, and in the decades following his death the early Church in Ireland deviated from Roman structures and developed into a largely independent organisation, commonly known as the Celtic Church. Structurally, the Celtic Church focused on autonomous monasteries rather than on bishoprics and dioceses. The founders of monastic settlements and their successors were usually clerics from an upper-class background; after their death, they were venerated as saints.

The monasteries resembled enclosed villages, with a guesthouse and a school, cells for the monks or nuns and dwellings for the clergy, with a refectory and small oratories or churches. Outside the monasteries, churches as such did not exist, and we can assume that religious service for the converted laity was rather irregularly held in the open air, probably at Christianised places of earlier significance.[4]

Spiritually, the Celtic Church was from her formative period distinguished by the co-existence of pagan practices and Christian traditions. In Ireland, the spread of the new faith happened as a rather slow and gradual process, mostly carried out by native clerics, or else by missionaries from a Celtic background. Thus, they would have had an intimate understanding of, and respect for, the ancient values and sacred sites – which might explain the scarcity of references to the destruction of pagan shrines in folklore, and the conspicuous absence of martyrs in early Irish history.

Characteristically, the missionaries of the early Celtic Church re-interpreted pagan symbols, ideas, and traditions in light of the new faith. Ancient rituals – among them the cult of wells, trees and stones – were allowed to continue much as before, though now under a Christian label, with the lore and venerations of saints replacing the cult of deities.

Ogham Stones and Stone Idols

Early Celtic religion and culture was characteristically aniconic and oral. Hence, the Celtic inhabitants of Ireland had initially no pictorial images of their deities but venerated the divine in the features of the physical landscape; and they transmitted their traditions, myths and laws exclusively by word of mouth, without developing a script.

Three-faced stone head, Woodlands, County Donegal

The human head played an important role in the religious life of the pagan Celts, and was considered the seat of the human soul and consciousness. Consequently, heads were a valuable and prestigious possession, and Celts preserved the skulls of their dead leaders as talismans and the heads of their enemies as war trophies. Continental Celts decorated vases with representations of human heads or sculptured them in stone. The earliest stone heads from Ireland date from the late Iron Age. Among the most magnificent examples are the three-faced heads from Corleck in County Cavan and from Woodlands in County Donegal.[5]

From about the fourth century AD, probably due to contacts with the Roman world, those traditional concepts began to change, and by the time of St Patrick's arrival in Ireland figural representations of deities and a distinctive script have already been established.

The earliest surviving iconic representations of the country were human heads, busts and full figures, carved from stone. Like the older ritual stones which had been decorated in the ornamental La Tène style, they belong exclusively to the northern half of the country.

When Christian missionaries arrived in the north, they apparently embraced the idea to transmit religious messages with carved figurines; their legacies are several unique sculptures from the transitional period between paganism and Christianity. As they combine Christian symbolism with an earlier iconographic tradition, they are extremely difficult to date and to interpret, and sometimes it is not possible to state whether a pagan deity, a mythical or historical king or a cleric is represented in the carving.[6]

Ogham-inscribed pillars belong predominantly to the south and south west of Ireland, where they occur in concentrations in Counties Cork, Kerry and Waterford. Since Ogham is based on the Latin alphabet, it is very likely that pre-Patrician Christians and an acquaintance with Roman culture had influenced the development of the script.

The Seven Deadly Sins, White Island, County Fermanagh

Monastic life on White Island started in about the fifth century AD; the surviving ruins stem from a twelfth-century Romanesque church. Since the early nineteenth century, eight stone figures had been discovered on the island, some of them built into the walls of the church with the carved sides inwards or downwards. After excessive discussions regarding their dating and interpretation, scholars agree now that they belong to the ninth or tenth century, and represent, except for the Sheela-na-Gig on the very left, either clerics or aspects of Christ.

In 1958, however, when only seven figures had been discovered, Macalister proposed a fanciful interpretation of the carvings as representations of the Seven Deadly Sins. From the left to the right, he described: lust, traditionally symbolised by a Sheela-na-Gig; laziness, sitting idly with hands in a muff; figure three had not been detected then; gluttony, represented by a person with one hand up to the mouth and a dinner knife in the other; greed, by a man carrying off stolen poultry; pride, fully adjusted with brooch and weapons and with nose in the air; anger might have been too horrifying, so the artist seems to have chipped the image off; and envy, finally, looks out from a window.[8]

Traditionally, the invention of Ogham is attributed to the mythical Oghma of the Tuatha Dé Danann. He is the Irish adaptation of Ogmios, the Gaulish God of eloquence, and was noted for his speech and poetry.[7] The script consists of sets of up to five strokes, which were marked along a central line, usually the sharp edge of a stone pillar, and were written from the bottom upwards, and, if necessary, downwards on the opposite side. Ogham is the earliest form of written Irish, and was in use from about the fourth until the seventh or eighth century.

The inscriptions are characteristically short, giving the name of a person and details of his ancestry. Ogham-inscribed pillars are certainly commemorative stones but their exact purpose remains unknown. Several stones were defaced or forcefully removed, and others were Christianised by the incision of a

Holed Ogham Stone of Kilmalkedar, County Kerry

The ruins of Kilmalkedar church are Romanesque, but monastic activity at the site began in the sixth or seventh century. Among various monuments from the early Christian period is a perforated Ogham-inscribed pillar in the graveyard. The stone is renowned for healing rheumatism and epilepsy, and patients would walk round the pillar three times while saying the prescribed prayers.[9]

cross, leading to assumptions that Ogham stems from a pagan background. But they might just as well have commemorated early converts or pilgrims, and only clerics under Patrician influence, coming from the north where Ogham was unknown, would later have regarded them a pagan threat.

Ogham stones attracted surprisingly little folklore. Only a few of these are credited with healing power, but even then would the inscriptions scarcely play a role in the rituals.[10]

Thorgrim's Stone, Killaloe, County Clare

A unique stone, dated to about 1,000 AD and bearing an Ogham and a runic inscription has been discovered in Killaloe in 1916. The Ogham inscription reads 'A blessing on Thorgrim'. The runes inform that 'Thorgrim carved this cross'. The Scandinavian runic script consisted of straight vertical or horizontal lines, carved into wood and stone. Irrespective of the similarities, it is not directly related to Ogham. Earliest examples date from the third century AD, when Scandinavia was still widely pagan. With the coming of Christianity, runes appear on memorial stones for the dead. The inscriptions would usually refer to a good deed performed for the benefit of the soul and invoke a blessing for the deceased.[11]

Pagan Idols and the Disempowerment of the Ancient Gods

'Tear down their altars, smash their sacred pillars, and destroy by fire their sacred poles, and shatter the idols of their gods.'

Deutronomy, 12

In the biographies of early Irish saints, the overcoming of pagan religions and their representatives was a motif of great popularity; the opponents of the Christian faith would primarily be cast as druids, but the traditions of St Patrick preserve also the memory of several Celtic deities who tried to prevent the spread of the new religion: the Caoranach or Corra, a female spirit who took on the shape of a serpent and was associated with Croagh Patrick and Lough Derg in County Donegal; the god Lugh who appears as the literary Crom Dubh or Crom Cruach; and the Bull God whom Patrick encountered in south Armagh.

Hagiographical literature and oral traditions abound with legends of Patrick and other saints successfully contesting and combating their pagan adversaries, often with their own magic means.[12] The narratives illustrate how saints took over sites of druidical significance and, by preaching, blessing and performing miracles, transformed them into Christian shrines; they also show that the instruction to destroy pagan sanctuaries, as contained in the Book of Deuteronomy, was normally not implied by early Christian missionaries in Ireland.[13] The destruction of the main pagan idol Cenn Cruaich or Crom Cruach, at Magh Sléacht, as related in a ninth-century biography of St Patrick, can be regarded an exception.

The Crom Cruach or Crom Dubh does not feature in mythology and it seems that the character was created by medieval hagiographers as a personification of heathendom, probably modelled on the image of the Anti-Christ, combined with aspects of an ancient deity.

The firm link of the Crom Dubh tradition with the harvest festival of Lughnasa suggests that the Celtic god Lugh was the archetype of the literary Crom Dubh.

Patrick's biographers relate that the saint destroyed the main idol of the Crom Dubh at Lughnasa. Thereby, the ancient harvest festival was transformed into a celebration of the Christian victory over paganism and should, among Irish speakers, become widely known as *Domhnach Chrom Dubh*, the Sunday of Crom Dubh.[14]

In popular tradition the Crom Dubh has retained the qualities of an ancient harvest god who dwells in the underworld and cares for the germination and growth of seeds. At Lughnasa, stone idols of the god were presented with flowers or fruit to acknowledge his role in the process of growth, and to ensure and maintain the fertility of the land. Often, this custom continued long after the particular stone had lost its initial link to the Crom Dubh. Elsewhere, as with the stone circle at Lough Gur, or with the Pagan Stone or Crom Cruach near Holywell, County Fermanagh, the name of the harvest god survived in folk memory until fairly recently.[15]

The Crom Cruach or the Killycluggin Stone, County Cavan

According to a medieval text, the idol of the Crom Cruach was a pillar decorated all over with gold, and standing in Magh Sléacht, surrounded by twelve stones, clad in silver and representing minor deities. It was at the time of Lughnasa when St Patrick approached the ritual site, and his mere presence made the stone circle sink into the ground, and the gilded pillar fall over. Not entirely satisfied with this victory, Patrick smashed the idol in an attempt to destroy it forever. Magh Sléacht translates 'plain of prostration' or 'plain of destruction', and has been identified with the Killycluggin area of County Cavan. In the vicinity of an overgrown circle of mostly prostrate stones, archaeologists have excavated two fragments of a decorated pillar with ornaments of the early Celtic La Tène style. The pillar has certainly been of ritual or religious significance, and it is obvious that it had been deliberately smashed. Curiously, local tradition attributes the destruction to an unnamed farmer, who – in about 1900 – wanted to rid the field of the obstruction; any association with St Patrick was decisively dismissed.[16]

Ronadh Crom Dubh, Lough Gur, County Limerick

The great stone circle at Grange, Lough Gur, is sometimes styled Ronadh or Rannach Chrom Dubh, the 'Staff of Crom Dubh'. The largest and almost square pillar was traditionally believed to be an idol of the Crom Dubh, which – in pagan times – used to speak and deliver oracles and divinations. Into the middle of the twentieth century it was customary to visit the Grange stone circle around the time of Lughnasa and to leave garlands of flowers on the pillar representing the Crom Dubh. Noteworthy is the alignment of the pillar with other ancient monuments around Lough Gur towards the sunrise at Lughnasa and the sunset at Samhain, emphasising the beginning and the end of autumn and stressing the link of the stone circle to the harvest season.[17]

In south Armagh, St Patrick reportedly encountered a pagan demon in the shape of a fierce bull. The concept of horned deities is ancient and possibly pre-dates the Celts in Ireland. Several Stone Age cultures linked the earth mother with a consort in the shape of a bull; Celtic and other Indo-European religions believed in cow goddesses, or in a land goddess and her bull lovers. For ancient Ireland, there is some material and iconographic evidence of the cult of a bovine deity. Court cairns, for instance, the earliest type of Neolithic structures, are commonly dubbed 'horned cairns' for their structural stones which form the outline of a horned bull's or cow's head. Some 330 court cairns exist in Ireland, the majority of them in Ulster and east Connacht. From the same regions stem several late Iron Age or early Christian carvings which seem to represent horned deities.[18]

Echoes of the veneration of horned deities appear in popular and literary traditions – again recorded primarily in the distribution area of court cairns. Bóinn was the white cow goddess connected with the river Boyne and the monuments of Newgrange; the Cailleach Bhéarra had a bull called the Tarbh Conraidh, who was so vigorous that every cow that heard his roar calved within a year; the Cailleach petrified her bull when he had annoyed her, and faint memories of that episode survive in folk-tales of a hag or female magician turning bulls into stones. In Kilross, County Sligo, for instance, the petrifaction of a bull is alternatively attributed to the Cailleach or to an anonymous celebrated magician.[19] The most obvious indication of the spiritual importance of bulls in Celtic Ireland, however, is the *Táin Bó Cuailnge*, the saga regarding the Cattle Raid of Cooley. Meadhbh,

St Patrick's Chair, Carrickatuke and Bull's Track, Ballymacnab, County Armagh

Popular lore in south Armagh relates that St Patrick had intended to build his main church of the north on the highest point of Carrickatuke ridge, about 10 miles from Armagh town. But night after night, a demon bull destroyed what Patrick had built during the day, until the saint was so annoyed that he left to found a church in Armagh instead. The bull jumped from Carrickatuke to Ballymacnab, next to Navan, and finally to Lisnadill; in all these places stones bearing imprints in the shape of hoof marks are said to mark the 'Bull's Track'. When the bull went mad at last, the people gathered to kill him. They buried him on top of Corran Hill, under the largest stone they could find. Known as the Grey Stone, the pillar was in earlier narratives also linked with the Donn Cuailnge, and said to mark the burial of the dark bull from the Táin.

A rude rock seat on Carrickatuke Ridge is pointed out as St Patrick's Chair. On Bilberry Sunday, local people used to come to the place, to collect bilberries and to sit in the Chair to make a wish. The date of the gathering, the former presence of a cairn, and the wishing seat allow assumption that Carrickatuke had once been an assembly site for the harvest festival of Lughnasa.[20]

queen of Connacht, desired to buy the famous Donn Cuailnge, the Brown Bull of Cooley in Ulster, to match her husband Ailill's bull Finnbheannach, the White Horned of Connacht. Her attempts failed, and she raised and led an army to seize the bull by force, thus initiating a war between the provinces of Connacht and Ulster. The *Táin* ends with a terrible fight between the two bulls; Donn was victorious, but died when he realised the extent of the slaughter and destruction in his name.[21]

The Petrified Sinners

With the defeat of the druids, the saints inherited some of their functions and with them the druidical knowledge of sorcery and magic. In the Christian context, acts of sorcery are considered miracles, and biographies of saints abound with them.

Among the magic powers attributed to druids was the ability to curse people or places through spells and incantations and to petrify their enemies. The most impressive manifestations of this notion are the rows of pillar stones at Carnac in Brittany, said to be one of Caesar's troops metamorphosed by Celtic druids.[22] In Scotland, Wales and England, numerous standing stones were popularly believed to be humans, petrified by druids. Irish folklore, too, has preserved several instances of druids or magicians turning their enemies into stone. Typically, their petrified opponents are said to have been giants, and the tales would have developed from the need to explain the origin of massive stone boulders.

References in hagiographical literature indicate that Irish saints too made extensive and effective use of their cursing potential, usually to prevent or punish crime. Consequently, the culprit would fall dead, or be swallowed by the earth. Sometimes, the saints' wrath did not even flag when punishing themselves for what they considered misconduct. County Cork tradition recalls the fate of young St Latiaran who used to go to the forge at Cullen for fire and to carry the embers home in her apron. One day the smith admired her beautiful feet, and in a moment of vanity the girl looked down on herself. Instantly the embers burnt a hole into her apron, and Latiaran unleashed the curse that never again should a smith's anvil be heard in Cullen. Thereafter, in an act of self-punishment, she sank into the ground, leaving a heart-shaped stone – the *Cloichín na Cúirtéise* or Curtsey Stone – to mark the spot

The False Men, Knocknafearbreaga, Clooney, County Clare

In 1892, the antiquarian Westropp recorded the current version of the tale of Knocknafearbreaga: 'The saint, who was building Tulla church, was too busy to cook. So he used to send his blessed bull to the monks of Ennis Abbey for food. There were seven thieves about this place in ancient times, and they went to rob the bull, but he roared so loud the saint heard him over in Tulla. He stopped building and knelt down, and he prayed and cursed at the one that was hurting his bull. The thieves were struck and became farbreags or sham men.' The story is still well remembered today in the area, though the number of the thieves has – corresponding to the surviving number of stones – reduced to three or four.[23]

of her disappearance. Into the twentieth century, local youths gathered at the stone for harvest celebrations around the start of July.[24]

The motif of petrifaction as an act of punishment – certainly related to the Biblical tradition of Lot's wife and her metamorphosis into a pillar of salt – occurs occasionally in medieval biographies of Irish saints, but became extremely popular in folklore. The twelfth-century biography of St Caillín, for instance, relates that he was confronted by the local chieftain Fearngna and his druids when he began to build a monastery at Fenagh, County Leitrim. On Caillín's prayer, the druids were turned into stone and the ground opened to swallow the king. When the Ordnance Survey visited Fenagh in 1836, folklore still linked that episode with the 'Long Stones', a group of Bronze Age pillars in the area.[25]

The church at Tulla, County Clare goes back to the seventh-century saint, Mochulla. His biographer informs that King Guire, in an attempt to prevent the saint from founding a church in his territory, sent

St Fiachna's Butter Lumps (left and opposite page)
and Petrified Woman (above) **Temple Feaghna,
Garranes, County Kerry**

*In the field just beyond the graveyard of Temple Feaghna
lies an impressive set of stones, locally known as the
Butter Stones or Butter Lumps. Their original purpose,
whether pagan or early Christian, is uncertain. From
nineteenth-century antiquarians' reports we learn that
pilgrims would traditionally visit Temple Feaghna and
the holy well at Easter time and, as the final ritual of
the pattern, turn the stones in their basins. The stones
are regarded as healing stones, and 'homing stones',
which would automatically return if removed. Local lore
attributes the origin of the Butter Stones to a miracle
performed by the sixth-century saint, Fiachna. Some
claim that a woman, employed by the saint to look after
his farm, had cheated on him and secretly sold his butter
at the market. Others say that local farmers complained
to Fiachna about a certain woman who owned no cows
herself but would set charms to get her neighbours'
milk profits. Anyway, Fiachna decided to look into the
matter, and when he called to the woman's house
unannounced he discovered seven large rolls of butter
on a rough block of wood. The furious saint cursed the
woman and turned the butter rolls, together with the
timber block, into stones. The unfaithful woman ran to
escape the saint's vengeance but Fiachna soon caught
up with her and petrified her too, leaving her a pillar
stone down by the river.[26]*

seven soldiers to arrest him. They slay Mochulla's tame bull but the saint eventually converted the soldiers to Christianity and they assisted him in building Tulla church. Popular tradition in east Clare had amended the hagiographical text and enriched it with the theme of the petrified culprits to explain the origin of a row of pillar stones on Knocknafearbreaga, the Hill of the False Men.

Three conspicuous stones near St Brendan's Well in Ventry, County Kerry, are linked to the tradition of the miracle of the Epiphany or visit of the Magi. It is said that on that night water would turn to wine, but people are not supposed to spy on this wonder, nor to take advantage of it. A local legend tells that the stones are the petrified remains of three friends who once ignored the sacred prohibition and attempted to drink from the wondrous wine.[27]

In an interesting variant of the theme, the curse of a saint turns rolls of butter into rounded 'butter stones'. Since the nineteenth century, scholars have reasonably speculated that 'butter stones' might have been parts of old dairies, or else played some role in magic observances to help with butter making. Only when their initial purpose was lost would the tales of the metamorphosis have been applied to explain the peculiar name.[28]

**Butter Stone at
St Peakaun's Shrine, Glen of
Aherlow, County Tipperary**
(left and opposite page)

*St Peakaun's is a small monastic
site in a quiet and peaceful setting,
just off the main Cahir to Tipperary
road. St Peakaun's Shrine was once
reputed to have matchmaking
qualities. Into the early decades
of the twentieth century, the place
was therefore popular with girls
wishing to marry soon. Founded
by the sixth century saint Abbán,
it became firmly linked to his
successor, St Peakaun or Béagán,
to whom the church, the well and
the circular cell are dedicated.
The centre of the cell is marked
by a bullaun stone with three
basins. One of them would always
contain some water and has –
according to local lore – formerly
been used as a baptism font. Older
sources claim that the basins
once held rounded stones, one of
which had been the famous
Butter Stone. It has long been an
object of great reverence, and is
today well protected from theft,
kept outside the ruined church.*

*The current story tells of how
St Peakaun once asked a local
woman for something to eat.
Although she was engaged in
butter making, she denied having
any food in the house. The saint
cursed her, transforming the
butter roll into a rounded stone,
which still bears the imprints
of her fingers.[29]*

The motif of petrified sinners who had dared to violate Sabbath or Sunday by entertaining themselves began to appear in oral tradition from the seventeenth or eighteenth century, when the keeping of the holy day became an issue for both the Reformed and the Catholic Church. Wherever stone circles occur in Europe, we can expect to find the tale of petrified dancers and their musicians attached to them. In Ireland, the motif occurs less frequently. It has only been recorded in a small area in the east of the country, and has in all likelihood been introduced from Cornwall and Wales where it is exceptionally widespread.[30]

Imprints in Stone

The durability and impenetrability of the material has certainly contributed to, if not initiated, the development of a cultic veneration of stones. Curious impressions on stone were often attributed to supernatural or superhuman characters, since they alone were held capable of altering the surface of stones by merely touching them, without the aid of tools. As previously mentioned, small circular indentations in standing stones are sometimes explained as the fingerprint of otherworld women or heroes. Footprints in stones, often complemented by other Bronze Age decorations, belong almost exclusively to the heroic tradition of mystic clan ancestors.

The hollows of bullaun stones, especially those of natural origin, are primarily ascribed to the actions of saints from the early Celtic Church in an effort to emphasise the might and power of the new faith. On a few occasions stones are said to have softened under the head of an infant, thus indicating a later religious vocation. More often, adult saints would have left the impressions of their hands and fingers, their feet and knees, their heads and sometimes backs while kneeling or sitting on stones, lying on rocks or leaning against boulders. Particularly prominent, especially in Leinster, are stones bearing the imprints of a saint's knees. They are often styled Gloonan Stones, a derivation from the Irish word *glúin* for knee.[31] The motif is recurrently set in the context of a saint's encounter with hostile pagans who try and prevent the spread of the new religion. The story regarding St Beaglaoch's Stone near Gortahork in County Donegal is characteristic. It tells of how the saint had to run for his life from the local pagan king. When Beoglaoch was eventually exhausted and unable to continue

**The Piper's Stones,
Athgreany, County Wicklow**
(opposite page)

The stone circle dates from the late Bronze Age and consists of fourteen boulders of local granite, some of them prostrate. There is a tradition that the Piper's Stones are named after bagpipe music that was played there by the fairies at midnight. More popular is the belief that the boulders had been a piper and young maidens, who ignored the Church's prohibition to dance on a Sunday. In a flash of lightning they were turned into stones. Similar stories are attached to other stone circles in the vicinity but had not been recorded elsewhere in Ireland.[32]

St Molua's Stone, Kyle, County Laois

The sixth-century saint Molua was educated at Bangor. He founded several monasteries in various parts of Ireland, before he finally settled in Kyle near Borris-in-Ossory to establish the monastery of Cluan Fherta Molua. Local lore relates that the saint initially used a large stone as a table to say Mass. When a druid had thrown that rock at Molua, the saint knelt down on it and prayed, leaving the imprints of his elbows, knees and head. At least one of the hollows would always contain some water, which has a cure for various ailments.[34]

St Brigid's Tears, Faughart, County Louth

The small hollows in two bullaun stones at St Brigid's Shrine in Faughart are said to be the marks of St Brigid's eye and tears, and have a cure for eye problems. The lore derives from a popular episode in a ninth-century biography of Brigid and explains her link to eye wells all over the country. The legend tells of how a man proposed to Brigid, and did not want to accept her refusal. The saint plucked one of her eyes out to make her less attractive to him. When her pursuer had angrily withdrawn, she miraculously restored her sight at a healing well.[35]

his flight, he threw himself down on his knees on a small boulder, wrapped his cloak around him and started to pray. Suddenly blackness descended, rendering the saint invisible to his pursuers and allowing him to escape, leaving only the impressions of his knees in the stone. The pagan king acknowledged the might of Christianity and asked Beaglaoch to baptise him.

Hagiography and folklore abound with similar stories of saints marking their presence in stones, and examples of imprint stones have been recorded from almost every part of Ireland. They are frequently situated near holy wells and early monastic sites, and are usually renowned for their healing virtues.[33]

Stone Boats

'Thus it is related, that people on the shore were astonished at the sight of the rock floating towards them with St Vogua alone on it, and that when he had landed in their presence the rock floated out to sea again, and directed its course back to Hibernia, whence it had come.'

John O'Hanlon (1875) [36]

A curious rock at the mouth of the Culdaff River in County Donegal is pointed out as St Buadan's Stone Boat. The story goes that Buadan and Colmcille once had to flee for their lives from hostile pagans in Scotland who wanted to prevent the saints from spreading the faith. Colmcille was the first to reach their boat – and hastily sailed off without waiting for his companion. Noticing the approaching pagans, Buadan fervently prayed to God for rescue – whereupon the rock the saint stood upon detached itself from the ground, and ferried him safely back to Ireland. [37]

To avail of stone boats when no other means of transport were at hand is a motif that features quite prominently in the biographies of early Irish saints. Popular tradition has often adapted this theme to explain the origin of conspicuous stones and rocks on the shores of rivers, lakes and the sea. Several stone boats survived to our day, though they have – as the result of being profaned – invariably lost their ability to float across the waters.

The stone boat near the airport on Inishmore

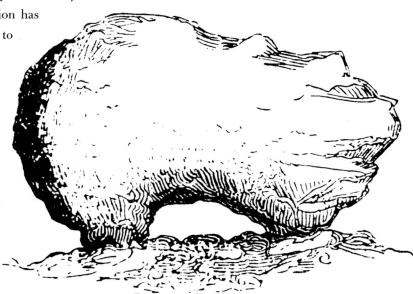

St Declan's Stone, Ardmore, County Waterford

The legend of St Declan's stone boat went almost unchanged from his twelfth-century biography into oral tradition. On his return from Rome, Declan visited St David in Wales; when he continued his journey to Ireland, he forgot his bell on a rock at the shore, and noticed the loss only when he had already sailed a considerable distance. Declan prayed to God for help, and the rock with the bell on took to the sea and followed Declan's boat. The saint, acknowledging the miracle, decided to let the stone lead the way, and built the church of Ardmore overlooking the shore where the stone boat has finally landed. [38]

St Barry's Stone Boat, Kilbarry, County Roscommon

Local tradition has it that St Barry arrived on the Longford side of the Shannon and wished to cross to Roscommon. When he could not find a boat, he stepped upon a large stone and floated across the river. In the 1830s, John O'Donovan was told that the people of the district continued to use the stone boat even after the saint's death; only when they lost their innocence did the stone boat sink. Other sources recall that the stone disappeared after a woman profaned it by beetling clothes on it. Early in the twentieth century, St Barry's stone boat has miraculously come back, and is since kept in the churchyard of Whitehall Church.⁴⁰

in County Galway belonged to St Enda and St Colmcille, who both used it to travel between the mainland and the Aran Islands; Colmcille has another boat in Glencolumbcille in County Donegal; St Barry's stone boat can be admired in Kilbarry in County Roscommon; St Declan's boat at Ardmore shore in County Waterford gained popularity as a healing stone, while St Mogue's from Temple Lake in County Cavan was once a notorious cursing stone; one portion of St Vogue's or Véoc's stone boat reportedly lies at the shore near Carn church in County Wexford. The sixth-century saint had safely travelled on the rock to Penmarch in Brittany, where it broke in two. One piece floated back to Ireland and the other, bearing the imprint of the saint's head, remained in Brittany, and is used there as a healing stone to relieve headaches and fever.³⁹

Mass Rocks and Penal Altars

Simple crosses incised in ancient stone monuments are a common feature throughout Ireland, and there is reason to believe that a good number of them had been carved by early Christian missionaries who had been keen to re-interpret pagan sacred sites in light of the new faith. Popular tradition would nevertheless prefer to date the incisions to the seventeenth and eighteenth centuries and regard the stones as Mass Rocks or Penal Altars of the Cromwellian period and the time of the Penal Laws.

Through Cromwell's conquest of Ireland in 1649, with the ensuing ruthless persecution of the Catholic clergy, the destruction of churches and monasteries, the deportation of bishops and regulars,

**An Altóir, Srahwee,
County Mayo**

*The Altóir at Sraith Bhuí or
Srahwee is actually a wedge
tomb from the late Neolithic
or early Bronze Age. A simple
cross has been carved in the
capstone to Christianise
the ancient monument.
Its isolated position in the
shelter of a small hillock
certainly influenced its choice
as a Penal Altar.[41]*

and the prohibition to celebrate Catholic Mass, Catholic worship became open-air affairs again, celebrated in secluded places by fugitive priests. When priests eventually got orders to register with the authorities to obtain permission to stay in the country, the vast majority – cautioned by the previous persecutions – preferred the risks of being sought out and continued to perform their duties secretly, in private homes or in the open, on Mass Rocks.[42]

Cromwell's death was followed by a short period of relative religious tolerance until, in the aftermath of the Battle of the Boyne in 1690 and the defeat of the Catholic King James II, the Protestant Parliament introduced a comprehensive body of suppressive laws, aimed to further diminish the rights of the Catholic population of Ireland. The laws became commonly known as Penal Laws, and accordingly the simple stone altars which again served for celebrating Mass were called Penal Altars.

Mass Rocks or Penal Altars occur in almost every county of Ireland but are particularly common in the west and north. Those located in the vicinity of holy wells or early monastic sites are primarily table-like structures, associated with the local patron saint; they were certainly altars from the times of the early Celtic Church, but may well have been objects of an even earlier veneration. Cross-inscribed monuments from the megalithic period occur often in isolated settings, and have characteristically no traditional links to particular saints.

Penal Altar, Tobernalt, County Sligo

The Mass Rock at Tobernalt (Tobar an Ailt) near Sligo town is constructed of several stones, with the top slab showing a number of small circular indentations. They are interpreted as the imprints of St Patrick's fingers, and it is locally believed that prayers said while holding the fingers in the impressions will be answered through the intercession of the saint. Folklore recalls that the altar was used as a Mass Rock during Penal Times, but the sanctity of the place reaches certainly further back. Tobernalt has been identified as an ancient Lughnasa assembly site; today, Mass is again celebrated at the altar on Garland Sunday, the last Sunday of July, and attracts a considerable number of devotees.[43]

Mass Rock, Edenmore, County Down

Locally known as the Mass Rock, the incision of a cross into the pillar stone is commonly ascribed to the times of Catholic persecutions. But the Edenmore Stone seems to be of earlier significance. Just as several similar pillars in the North, it has formerly been whitewashed in springtime. The reasons are no longer remembered, but it is possible that the custom was-like that of the White Stone of Calliagh Beri in the Slieve Gullion area of South Armagh – related to the fertility of livestock and crops.[44]

PART II

Rituals — Religious, Social, Spiritual

Stones of Kingship

'They used to place him that shall be their captain upon a stone, always reserved for that purpose, and placed commonly upon a hill, on many of which I have seen the foot of a man formed and graven which they say was the measure of their first captain's foot, whereon he standing receiveth an oath to preserve all the former ancient customs of the country inviolable.'

Edmund Spenser, *A View of the Present State of Ireland* (sixteenth century)[1]

Celtic communities were based on clans or *tuatha*, ruled by local chieftains and provincial priest kings; the national or high kingship of Ireland was introduced during medieval times. Chieftains and kings were selected from the leading families and installed at specific inauguration places, which were usually the main assembly or palace sites of their respective territories. It appears that the Celts, when choosing the locations for these prestigious sites, preferred places of earlier spiritual significance, distinguished by cairns, burial mounds and other Bronze Age monuments, which they linked to their own mythical ancestors. They would have added specific insignia of power, however, and frequently furnished their inauguration sites with sacred trees and highly venerated stones, which represented territorial power and kingship.[2] The inaugural ceremony of a Gaelic chieftain was known as *banais rige,* the king's wedding, and was considered his symbolical marriage to the sovereignty of the territory or the entire island. In folklore and medieval literature sovereignty appears under different names, but she is always the personified goddess of the land. By her marriage to a king, she hands over the responsibility for the prosperity of the realm. There were certainly substantial local variations of the ritual cohabitation rites; medieval historical and literary sources, however, suggest that inaugural stones might have served as channels for the king to connect with the sovereignty of the land.

St Columb's Stone, Belmont/Derry, County Derry

With the introduction of Christianity, inauguration rites and stones came under the spiritual protection of the new faith. The Tripartite Life, for instance, relates that St Patrick paid a visit to Grianan of Aileach in County Donegal, and 'left there a certain stone, blessed by him, upon which the promised kings and princes should be ordained'. In 1837, the Ordnance Survey registered a conspicuous flagstone in the gardens of Belmont House, north of Derry city. The flag, locally known as St Columb's Stone and believed to be the former inauguration stone of the O'Doherty clan, is very likely identical with the inauguration stone from Patrick's biography.[3]

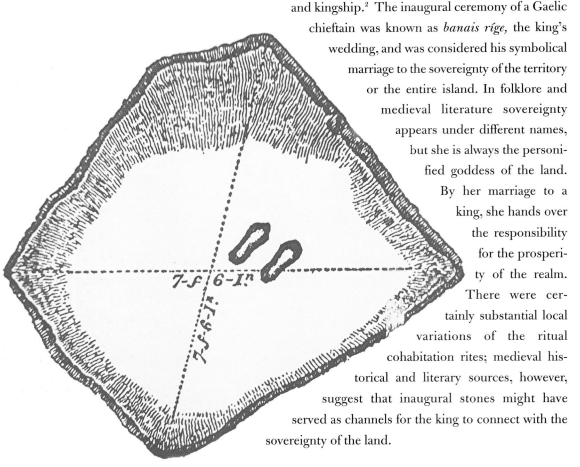

Towards the end of the thirteenth century, the system of Gaelic kingship began to decline and was gradually replaced by lordship and earldom. Celtic inauguration rites did not particularly appeal to the incoming Norman gentry, and only the Bourkes made a political concession to native practice when they formally inaugurated the heads of both their Mayo and their Galway branch.[4] In the early seventeenth century, the English conquest eradicated Gaelic kingship altogether; numerous inauguration sites with their furniture were destroyed or fell into oblivion. Some of these long-forgotten sites have recently been re-discovered by historians and archaeologists.

Royal Pillars on the Hill of Tara

Especially well documented are the inaugural ceremonies at the Hill of Tara, one of the most important political and spiritual centres of Celtic Ireland. Initially a burial place of Neolithic and Bronze Age people, and mythically linked with the Indo-European land goddess Tea, Celtic tribes made the Hill of Tara the assembly place for the celebration of Samhain, one of the major festivals of the Celtic calendar. Moreover, Tara became the inauguration site and royal residence of local kings. The power of the kings of Tara would gradually rise, until they were the most influential ones in the country and established the national or high kingship of Ireland.[5]

From a medieval text regarding the inauguration of King Conaire Mor, we learn of the important role of the sacred royal pillars at Tara: wearing a cloak that would only fit a true king, Conaire had to drive a chariot drawn by horses that only a worthy applicant to kingship could control. Arriving at Tara, he had to pass the final ordeals. 'There were two flagstones at Tara, called Blocc and Bluigne, which stood so close together that one's hand could only pass sideways between them. When they accepted a man, they would open before him until his chariot went through. And Fál was there, the "stone penis" at the head of the chariot-course. When a man should have the kingship, it screeched against his chariot axle, so that all might hear.'[6]

The authenticity of the *Lia Fáil* has not always been undisputed. The controversy arises from a Scottish tradition, which claims that their Stone of Scone would actually be the genuine *Lia Fáil*. The Irish historian and poet, Geoffrey Keating, writing in the seventeenth century, relates that about the year 513, Fergus, heir to the Scottish throne, sent to his brother Mortough, then king of Ireland, for the stone so he could be crowned king of Scotland on it. Fergus, however, failed to return the celebrated

Inauguration stones on the Hill of Tara, County Meath. The Lia Fáil (right) **Blocc and Bluigne** (opposite page)

According to the twelfth-century Dindshenchas, the Hill of Tara had originally four famous stones, namely, Moel to the east, Blocc to the south, Bluigne to the north, and the Lia Fáil to the west.[7] Moel has vanished, and it is uncertain whether it played any part in the inaugural ceremony. Blocc and Bluigne formed the mythical gateway to the crowning site. With one pillar rather small and rounded, and the other tall and sharp-topped, they are a beautiful example of the female and male principle in gateway stones. The female aspect of the tall pillar, which is also known as St Adamnán's cross, is further stressed by the weathered carving of a Sheela-na-Gig. Women wishing to conceive would still rub the image as a talisman.[8]

A short distance from the gateway stones stands Bod Forghasa, the phallic granite pillar in the characteristic shape of Celtic Iron Age monuments. Phallic inauguration stones occur also in Scotland, and stood in several ancient royal residences of India, where they were considered the abodes of the essence of sovereignty. The stone on Tara Hill is named after Fergus, a fictional hero of the Ulaidh people who, myths reveal, had extraordinary virility.[9] More popularly, the pillar is said to be the legendary Lia Fáil, one of the wondrous gifts of the Tuatha Dé Danann to Ireland. They had endowed the stone with the ability to roar in order to indicate its approval of a legitimate king, but the birth of Christ silenced the pillar.[10]

stone; it was later transferred to the Abbey of Scone in Perth, and remained – now dubbed Stone of Scone or Stone of Destiny – for centuries the inaugural stone of Scottish kings. From about 1300, when the English king Edward I had seized the prestigious pillar, the Stone of Scone was kept under the seat of the coronation chair in Westminster Abbey. In 1996, the British government decided to return the stone to the people of Scotland; it is since on exhibition in Edinburgh Castle.[11]

Leaca na Ríogh – The Flagstones of the Kings

The descriptions of the inaugural rituals on the Hill of Tara are probably echoes of special ceremonies reserved for the establishment of the national kings of Ireland. Elsewhere there are no references to pillars gaining or refusing access to the crowning place, or to stones announcing their approval of a king by a roar.

Historical texts, as well as folk memory, recount that installation rites would usually have reached their climax when the newly-elected Gaelic king or chieftain mounted a specially designated inaugural flagstone and proclaimed to the assembly that he would rule righteously and honourably. The custom to install leaders while they stood on stones was once widespread; the practice had been carried out in ancient Athens and Scandinavia, and in Celtic contexts by the Picts of Scotland, and the Noricans in the Austrian province of Carinthia.[12]

In Ireland the most frequent term used for an inauguration stone is *leac* or flagstone, as in *Leac Mhic Eochadha*, which belonged to the Uí Chinnsealaigh; *Leac na Ríogh*, the Flagstone of the Kings where the O'Neills of Tyrone were crowned; or *Leac Cothraide* on the hill of Cashel. These stones are lost, and so is the flagstone of the MacMahons that gave the name to the townland of Leck in County Monaghan.

Several inaugural flagstones showed indentations resembling human feet. The ancient Celts did not care whether the imprints were carved into the stone by the Bronze Age creators of rock art, or caused naturally by erosion. To them, the marks were footprints left by the mythical ancestors of leading septs. Myths would characteristically relate that those ancestors lay with the personified goddesses of the land, and it is possible that a chieftain or king, when stepping into the ancestral footprint as part of his instalment, symbolically renewed the bond with the goddess. Examples of foot-marked inauguration stones survived in Cadamstown, County Offaly, near Warrenpoint, County Down, and at Carnfree, County Roscommon, and are linked to the O'Flanaghan, the Maginnis or MacGuinness, and the O'Conor clan respectively.[13]

The Proclamation Stone, Carnfree, County Roscommon

The small Bronze Age mound of Carnfree, reputedly the burial place of the mythical Connacht hero Fraoch, was the inauguration place of the royal Ó Conchobhair sept of Connacht. The deep marks on their inaugural stone, today known as the Proclamation Stone, are explained as the footprints of Conn Céadchathach or Conn of the Hundred Battles, the legendary ancestor and king of the Connachta. As part of the ceremony, newly-elected kings had to step in their bare feet into Conn's footmarks, before they had the inaugural insignia – sandals, a mantel and a wand – placed on them.

In 1641, at a time when Gaelic kingship had practically ceased to exist, Charles O'Conor, Don of Ballintubber, was the last Connacht king to be inaugurated at Carnfree. The Proclamation Stone has since been removed and is today preserved at Clonalis House near Castlerea.[14]

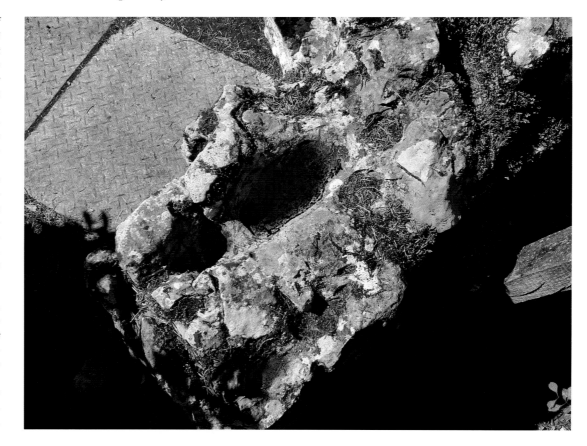

The Coronation Chairs of the O'Neills

In Irish popular tradition, natural or artificial stone chairs belong to otherworld women or to the festival of Lughnasa and St Patrick. In the contexts of kingship and inauguration, they appear conspicuously seldom, and were probably a later development influenced by the idea of coronation chairs from abroad.

Medieval maps of Tullahogue in County Tyrone show *Leac na Ríogh*, the inaugural stone of the O'Neills of Tyrone, as a stone throne with back and armrests. The term *leac* however, clearly implies a flagstone and not a seat or throne. Perhaps additional stones had been propped up against the original flag at a later stage, when crowning chairs had become fashionable. The last king installed on *Leac na Ríogh* was the Great Hugh O'Neill, Earl of Tyrone. Shortly after his defeat in 1602, Lord Mountjoy destroyed the stone chair to emphasise his victory and the ensuing end of Gaelic rule in Ireland.[15] Another stone chair survived and was discovered in the eighteenth century on Castlerea Hill, once the principal residence of the Clandeboy branch of the O'Neill sept. Though there is no definite evidence on the original purpose of the stone seat, it is popularly regarded as the inauguration chair of their chieftains.

The Inauguration Chair of Clandeboy, Castlerea Hill, County Down

The chair-like block of whinstone was apparently thrown from its elevated position, and remained unnoticed until about 1750, when it was built into the walls of the Belfast butter market. For almost a century, people used the stone for a convenient seat. With the demolition of the wall went the stone chair. Fortunately, it was rescued from a heap of rubble, and was later acquired by the Belfast Museum.[16]

Stones of Truth and Justice

'The truth is bitter sometimes, says the stone speaking in the earth.'

Old saying, recorded by Mr and Mrs Hall (1841)[1]

Oracle Stones of Ancient and Modern Ireland

Stones that roar or speak with a human voice appear to have their roots in the ancient animistic traditions of spirited nature. Unlike the closely related, but silent, swearing stones, speaking stones have no Christian links, and feature characteristically in the context of divination and oracles.

If we accept folklore as proof, there must have been several oracle stones in pre-Christian Ireland which spoke with human voice or uttered distinctive roars. The most prominent among them was certainly the *Lia Fáil*, the legendary inauguration stone at Tara, which used to announce its approval

Cloch Óir, the Golden Stone, Clogher, County Tyrone

Local tradition holds that Conchobhar mac Nessa had consulted the oracle stone of Clogher, which advised him to get a magical spear, sword, and shield in order to gain the sovereignty of Ulster. In 1490, a commentary on the registry of Clogher notes that 'this sacred stone is preserved at Clogher, on the right side into the church, and that traces of the gold which it had been formerly covered by the worshippers of the idol called Cermand Cestach are still visible'. Today, nothing remains of these traces of gold, and it is questionable if the pillar pointed out as the Cloch Óir is actually the original one.[2]

of a new king by crying out load. The Golden Stone of Clogher in County Tyrone was the highly renowned oracle of the north; since Clogher was the ancient centre of the kingdom of Oriel, the Golden Stone might well have played its role in the inauguration ceremonies of the local kings.

Popular tradition holds that most pagan oracle stones lost their speech with the arrival of Christianity. A few, nevertheless, continued to raise their voices at certain occasions into recent times. Clochlourish (*Cloch Labhrais*) near the Deehan River in County Waterford was a rather contemporaneous speaking stone, renowned for its judgements of right or wrong. Local lore recalls that a couple once asked the stone to establish whether the wife was unfaithful to the husband. The woman made her lover stand on a distant hill, and asked the stone to confirm that she would no longer have an affair with anyone than with the man on that faraway hill. On the wickedness of the woman, the stone split, and from the cleft came the words 'The truth is bitter sometimes'. The tale was current in the nineteenth century; some people claimed that this had been the only occasion on which the stone spoke with a human voice, while others insisted that Clochlourish gave all its oracles by speaking, until it split and fell silent.[3]

The Speaking Stones at Farranglogh near Oldcastle in County Meath, felt insulted in about 1800 when a man had ignored the prohibition to consult them twice in the same matter. Never since were the pillars heard to speak with human voice again. Another story regarding the same set of stones reflects the sacred prohibition to interfere with ancient monuments. It tells that long ago a steward to the landlord had ordered his labourers to remove the stones. Afraid of the consequences, they refused; infuriated to see his orders ignored, the steward himself began to smash the stones with a sledgehammer – and while he watched the first pillar collapsing, the man got notice that one of his children had just drowned.

Clocha Labharta – The Speaking Stones, Farranglogh, County Meath

In 1873, Eugene Conwell described the Clocha Labharta and noted that '... in the traditions of the neighbourhood, it is even yet current that they have been consulted; that they are infallibly effective in curing consequences of the "evil eye"; and that they were deemed to be unerring in naming the individual through whom these evil consequences came. Even up to a period not very remote, when anything happened to be lost or stolen, these stones were invariably consulted; and in cases where cattle, etc., had strayed away, the directions they gave for finding them were considered as certain to lead to the desired result. There was one peremptory inhibition, however, to be scrupulously observed in consulting these stones, viz., that they were never to be asked to give the same information a second time.'[4]

Oaths, Ordeals and the Touchstone to All Evil-Doers

Bishop Dive Downes when visiting County Cork in the year 1700, noted in his diary: 'I went to Kineigh: the parish stands three miles distant from Ballymoney to the NNW. A stone is in the SW corner of the Church of Kineigh counted very sacred which the Irish solemnly swear upon.'[5]

The custom of swearing an oath on sacred objects occurs in numerous cultures around the world, with the respective religious beliefs determining the choice of these objects. Among pagan Indo-European peoples, oaths on sacred stones were widespread and are just another expression of their belief in the magic qualities of stone.

There is no direct evidence, however, for the practice to swear oaths on stones in pre-Christian Ireland, though the custom is undeniably related to the ceremonial visit to ancient speaking stones and royal stone oracles. It seems that early missionaries have adapted the ancient concept of truth-finding stones, and allowed it to continue under a Christian prefix. Hence, Ireland's 'swearing stones' are invariably linked to saints of the Celtic Church, to whom they reputedly owe their special virtues. In folk tradition, these stones would often bear individual names, or are else known as Stones of Justice or Stones of Truth. The expression swearing stones is a rather recent term of convenience established by antiquarians, and used here to distinguish stones to swear on from the closely-related speaking and cursing stones.

In our Irish contexts, oaths sworn on stones were de facto ordeals to determine the truth or falsehood of disputed arguments, or to clear the name of an accused person by revealing the real culprit. The practice built on the notion that people swearing falsely would inevitably suffer some dreadful punishment, while those telling the truth would remain unharmed. Suddenly arising storms and tempests were often taken as an indication that a swearing stone was about to work its magic.

The practice to swear on stones co-existed with the oath on religious objects – preferably croziers, bells or the relics of saints – well into the nineteenth century, and fulfilled a social utility during times when legal aid was practically not available to wide sections of the population. Swearing stones were particularly popular in the west of Ireland. One of the most famous examples was St Fechin's Stone at Dooghta, County Galway, once feared as 'the touchstone and terror to all evil-doers'. Instructed by a guardian, people used to pray and turn the stone in order to clear their names from accusations. Local lore relates that a great sinner, afraid of being brought before the stone to swear his innocence, had thrown St Fechin's Stone into a bog hole. Years later, the man repented and prayed to God to help him recover the stone. His prayers were answered and St Fechin's Stone re-emerged from the bog. The sacred stone was preserved in Cong with a cross erected on its top until it was eventually stolen and has never been seen again.[6]

From the second half of the nineteenth century the tradition to swear on stones declined significantly. Apart from the influence of the Church, who no longer condoned 'superstitious' practices, the decline must also be accredited to courts which gradually replaced magic means when it came to establish the truth and to settle arguments. Subsequently, local Church authorities had ordered the removal of numerous swearing stones; from several reports telling how such stones had 'mysteriously' disappeared, we can gather that those orders were preferably carried out secretly. Leac Bhreacháin in Kilbrickan, County Galway, once a popular resort for people wishing to clear their names in disputes, is among the swearing stones that had vanished overnight. It is still told in the area that when Leac Bhreacháin had got a bad reputation as a 'cursing stone', it was deeply offended and took off through the air.[7]

**Leac na Naomh,
Caher Island, County Mayo**

The annual pilgrimage to Caher Island takes place on 15 August and is still very popular. After a visit to the holy well, pilgrims would congregate around the remains of an early monastic site, where Mass is said at the stone altar in front of the ruined church. Inside the church walls on another stone altar rests an impressive conglomerate known as Leac na Naomh, the Flag of the Saint.

Today Leac na Naomh is often referred to as a 'cursing stone', though there are no memories of its actual implication in malevolent or revengeful rituals. Its initial function shines through in an account given in 1838 by John O'Donovan for the Ordnance Survey. He notes that people who felt wronged or were openly scandalised would resort to Leac na Naomh 'to elicit the truth … They first fast and pray at home for a fixed time, imploring that God, through the intercession of Patrick and the other saints who blessed the flag, would bring about some occurrence which would show that they were wronged'. They would then sail to the island and turn Leac na Naomh, whereupon the weather would immediately become unfavourable, and some event would point out the real offender or culprit.[8]

**Swearing Stone,
Castledermot, County Kildare**

*In the grounds of the ruined
ninth-century monastery of
Disert Diarmada we find a
holed granite cross-slab, which
is popularly known as a
swearing stone or Leac na
Mionn, the Stone of the Oath.
Apart from its name, neither
historical references nor folklore
accounts from the area contain
any further information on the
stone. The perforation of the
slab and the situation of the
stone in an area of former Viking
influence suggest that it may
actually have been a contract
stone, linked to the Oath of
Odin, rather than a swearing
stone in the strict sense.[9]*

Doughmakeon Maltese Cross, County Mayo

In the middle of the nineteenth century, a cross-decorated slab was discovered and re-erected in the dunes of Doughmakeon. Nothing definite is known today about that particular pillar, but earlier folklore accounts of a virtuous swearing stone in the area seem to refer to the conspicuous find. In 1838, Caesar Otway took note of Duac McShaun's Stone, a flagstone on the sandy shore that used to be well guarded during harvest time for fear that its misuse might cause unfavourable weather. The flag was regarded as a swearing or cursing stone, and Otway relates that it was cast into the sea by a man notorious for his bad character, who feared the revelation of his deeds through the stone. In a folklore account from the 1930s, the slab would feature again, this time dubbed the 'Druid's Stone', which would bring about terrible storms if used for turning the sand in the dunes. This account blames a priest for having thrown the slab into the sea in the 1830s; the Druid's Stone, however, re-emerged, and was successfully turned in 1938 by a man who wanted to prove the unbroken power of the stone over the weather. O'Donovan of the Ordnance Survey finally informs that a blue slate, called Claidhimhín Chathasaigh or St Cathasach's Little Sword, stood once at the shores of Lough Cathasaigh not far from the Doughmakeon dunes. The slab was valued as a swearing stone to settle disputes until a local priest cast it into the sea.[10]

Cursing Stones and Protective Idols

It is, as the example of *Leac na Naomh* has shown, often impossible to draw a clear and distinctive line between cursing and swearing stones, as both their functions and purposes are closely related. The main distinguishing feature is perhaps that the use of swearing stones had focused on the determination of truth and justice, while the use of cursing stones had primarily aimed at the prevention or punishment of injustice. Only a few rather recent sources should claim that cursing stones had occasionally been abused and applied out of spite. These stories seem to be misinterpretations rather than reflections of a genuine popular custom and are very doubtful, given the common understanding that any curse, once unleashed, would fall, and inevitably hit the applicant if her or his cause were not morally justified.

Like swearing stones, cursing stones and protective idols seem to be a feature of the north and west of Ireland, particularly of the coastal areas. The threat to turn the stones against somebody was nevertheless more widespread and common even in areas where no such stones existed.[11]

St Brigid's Cursing Stone, Killinagh, County Cavan

Commentators would often assign the origin of the custom to druidic maledictions and incantations, but there is no reliable literary evidence that the druids had actually turned stones to curse people or places. Folklore associations of cursing stones with druids are scarce, and date exclusively from the early twentieth century onwards. They did possibly derive from the often quoted verse in Ferguson's poem on the death of Cormac mac Airt, which relates how the druids '… loosed their curse against the king, they cursed him in his flesh and bones, and daily in their mystic ring they turn'd the maledictive stones'. Ferguson composed his poem in 1865, at a time when it was highly fashionable to attribute ancient customs and monuments to the druids.[12]

The seventeenth-century biography of St Maedoc or Mogue of Ferns, copied from an older text, contains the earliest reliable reference to a cursing stone in Ireland. 'There is a stone of Maedoc in the place [i.e. Killybegs, County Fermanagh] on which he left this as one of its virtues, that whoever shall do wrong or injustice to the *erenaghs* or tenants of this church shall not be alive at the end of a year, if this stone be thrice turned widdershins against him, as the wise men of that land and territory agree.'[13]

The Killybegs stone is lost, but the saint left another, still existent cursing stone near his birthplace in County Cavan.

From medieval biographies of saints to twentieth-century folklore accounts, cursing stones and protective idds are characteristically linked to saints, early monastic settlements or holy wells. Occasionally referred to as 'Blessed Stones', they are more frequently named after the saints who bestowed them with their special virtues. The designation 'cursing stones' appeared from the late nineteenth and early twentieth century onwards in antiquarian reports. It is since used in archaeological, historical and folklore studies, but did not make its way into popular tradition.

To release the power of the stones, it was sometimes customary to prepare spiritually by fasting. Generally, applicants would recite the prescribed prayers – occasionally backwards – and finally turn the stones anticlockwise. The custom of sweeping cursing stones against somebody was exceptional, and has only been recorded at Ballyboy in County Cavan, and at Carrickmore in County Tyrone.[14]

Although other forms occur as well, the most common type of cursing stones were large, rounded pebbles lying on dry-stone altars called *leachta* or on altar-like natural boulders. The concept of 'cursing altars' is apparently based on the Old Testament, which relates that Moses and Elijah built altars of stone to curse the enemies of the Faith.[15]

There is evidence that several 'cursing stones' were used both for destructive and benevolent purposes. The desired effect depended on the direction of the turn. Thus, St Molua's Stone at his well in Drumeland, County Armagh, was formerly turned clockwise to promote good luck, or anticlockwise to evoke misfortune on others. St Colmcille supposedly left *Cloch Thoraigh* or the Tory Stone to the people of Tory Island, County Donegal, to protect themselves in times of danger. Folk memory recalls a few instances of people turning *Cloch Thoraigh* in the benevolent clockwise direction, but reports of its anticlockwise application predominate, and illustrate that it was repeatedly very successful in helping to avenge acts of injustice. The Tory Stone gained extreme popularity in 1884, when the British gunship *Wasp* sank on its way to the island to collect rents for an absentee landlord. The admiralty blamed a navigational error; the islanders attributed the incident to the Tory Stone. During a terrible storm towards the end of the century, a big wave swept *Cloch Thoraigh* into the sea.[16]

Very few cursing stones survive into our day. Church authorities have always fervently opposed their use; from the second half of the nineteenth century, the Catholic Church had sufficient power to end such practices. Several cursing stones were destroyed, whilst others were built into the walls of newly-erected churches to prevent people from ever turning them again with malevolent intentions. Inserted into the masonry of Ballina Cathedral in County Mayo are the fragments of the notorious cursing stone from Kilcummin. Locally it is firmly believed that at least one piece of the stone had been saved in time, and a few people would still know its whereabouts.[17]

Especially on the islands off the west coast, there is still a vague memory of stones that were once highly valued protective idols. People, however, are very reluctant to talk about the veneration of these stone idols, and only little bits of information would be passed on. About the God-stone from Garnish in County Cork, for instance, we know only that it resembles a human body, and used to be clad at certain times of the year. It seems to have disappeared, though there are allegations that it is still secretly cared for in the traditional manner.[18]

More information is available about the *Naomhóg*, the Little Saint of Inishkea North, County Mayo. The idol had been a small stone image, which every house on the island kept for a year in rotation. It had been dressed in homespun clothes, warmed by the fireside and put into a comfortable bed whenever its service was needed. In 1853, John E. Howard noted in *The Island of the Saints*, that any person who wants immediate revenge for an insult would resort to the *Naomhóg* and 'turn it round three times, and pray that his enemies might not prosper or get length of life; and their means would melt away like snow before the sun; their days would be shortened until in the end they would get a miserable death; in fact it is a stone that would put an end to bad people in a short time'.[19]

As the *Naomhóg* was also considered to have power over the weather, the islanders used her to evoke favourable winds, but likewise to raise storms when they felt endangered by invaders. Popular lore relates that a pirate who happened to survive a tempest created with the help of the *Naomhóg* had eventually smashed the idol; when the man fell almost immediately after his deed and severed his spine, it was attributed to the vengeance of the Little Saint. The islanders collected the pieces of the *Naomhóg* and wrapped them in a suit of flannel. Though the idol should never re-gain her full power over the elements, she was still regarded as the protectress of the island. In the early decades of the nineteenth century, a new parish priest on the island decided to end the practice. He threw the fragments of the idol into the sea, and burnt her suit. The priest soon met a premature death; the islanders, however, rescued the head of the *Naomhóg*, and some believe it is still carefully hidden on Inishkea.[20]

St Mogue's Floating Stone, Ballyboy, County Cavan

St Mogue or Maedoc of Ferns was born on a small island in Templeport Lake. There was no priest on the island to baptise the child, and no boat available to cross the lake, so his parents placed their newborn son on a large flagstone, which duly floated over to the shore, to have him christened. Local lore has it that the stone was for centuries used to ferry coffins over to the graveyard on the island. Only when it had been profaned – some say by a courting couple that went out on the stone, others blame a man for behaving indecently while he accompanied a coffin – did St Mogue's Stone break. One part sank; a second floated back to the island; a third fragment, which shows the imprint of the saint's head, reached the mainland, and was swept clean on a few occasions in order to work a curse in revenge for evictions. To stop the practice without destroying the sacred stone, the parish priest brought it into Kildoe church; today, it is used as a holy water font in the modern Ballyboy church, and its former reputation as a cursing stone is hardly remembered.[21]

Clocha Breacha, The Speckled Stones of Inishmurray, County Sligo
(left and opposite page)

In 1779, Gabriel Berenger visited Inishmurray. He wrote, 'If any one is wronged by another, he goes to this altar, curses the one who wronged him, wishing such evil may befall him, and turns one of the stones; and if he was really wronged, the specified evil fell on his enemy; but if not, on himself, which makes them so precautionate that the altar is become useless'.
The Clocha Breacha rest on a specially designated dry stone altar within the monastic enclosure of Inishmurray. The magnificent ensemble consists of about 70 rounded stones, some of them decorated with carved crosses, others featuring a cavity closed by a stone plug. Folklore relates that it is impossible to reckon the exact number of the stones; it is nevertheless considered unlucky to remove a single Speckled Stone from the altar, and local historian, Joe McGowan, recalls that a tourist had recently returned the one which he had previously taken from the island as a souvenir. The chain of accidents and bad luck became too much to bear.
Island tradition recalls that the cursing ritual on Inishmurray had to be preceded by a fast. Some claim it was then necessary to do the entire pilgrimage with its sixteen stations backwards; others relate that it was sufficient to walk around the altar 'lefthandwise', that is, against the course of the sun. The crucial part was the subsequent turning of the stones in an anticlockwise direction. According to island lore, the Clocha Breacha were last turned in the 1940s to successfully evoke a curse on Adolf Hitler.[22]

St Brigid's Stone, Killanagh, Tullyhaw, County Cavan
(right and opposite page)

On the roadside between Killinagh and Blacklion, overlooking Upper Lough MacNean, stands a contemporary sculpture called the 'Forum'. Unknown to most passers-by, it is a modern interpretation of St Brigid's Stone, which lies not far from the sculpture between the lakeshore and the ruined parish church of Killinagh.

Though twentieth-century sources would sometimes refer to St Brigid's Stone as a 'wishing chair', it had once a reputation as a cursing stone, and the pebbles in the basins would have been turned to unleash curses and maledictions. The task was considered very risky, for to let one single stone slip would have caused the curse to hit the applicant instead of the intended victim. In 2004, St Brigid's Stone was covered in moss and lichen, and it is obvious that it has not been resorted to for a long time.[23]

Stones of Love and Fertility

'If a woman proves barren, a visit with her husband to Darby and Grane's bed certainly cures her.'

Hely Dutton, *A Statistical Survey of the County of Clare* (1808)[1]

Among the different features of the sacred landscape, one would primarily associate fertility with springs and wells. Water as the source of life is highly revered all around the world and customs like bathing in certain wells in order to conceive or to heal female complaints are widespread. A link of stones to fertility is not at all obvious – stones are not nourishing, vitalising or refreshing. It is rather surprising therefore to find stones employed in various types of fertility-associated rituals – semi-magic rites to find a partner, ceremonial marriage vows, and practices to facilitate conception and to assist in childbirth.

In Irish tradition, childbirth stones would characteristically appear in Christian contexts, linked to saints and early monastic settlements. Stones with aphrodisiac or fertility-promoting connotations, on the other hand, are predominately monuments from the megalithic period, or else medieval variations of the basic idea that lies behind the ancient concepts. The same pattern prevails throughout Atlantic Europe in all the former strongholds of megalithic cultures. From Scandinavia down to Spain and Portugal, popular lore would apply myths of fertility goddesses or virile heroes to Stone Age structures and Bronze Age pillars, and subsequently apply them in rituals and ceremonies to increase fertility in people, livestock and crops. In Central Europe, where megaliths are scarce or absent, such rituals had been carried out at cup-marked Bronze Age boulders and pre-Christian basin stones.

Stone Magic to Find a Partner

Well into the twentieth century, a single person did not hold an equal status to one who had spouse and children, and memories of practical jokes played on unmarried men and women reflect the communal disapproval of their status. Since the traditional time for weddings in rural Ireland was Shrovetide, the unfortunate people who were not married by then became victims of public mockery, particularly during Lent. In Munster and south-west Leinster, the first Sunday in Lent was known as Chalk Sunday, from the custom to mark singles with a piece of chalk; in parts of Connacht ashes or salt were sprinkled on them. Such practical jokes were not just a peculiarity of the countryside; in 1814, when Mr and Mrs Hall visited Waterford city, they noticed that on Ash Wednesday unmarried women and men sitting on logs of wood were dragged through the streets of the town. Throughout the nineteenth century, a similar, though more elaborate ritual, has been customary in nearby Ardmore.[2]

With the prospect of disrespect and mockery, it is not surprising to find unmarried people engaging in a variety of semi-magic practices, which promise to facilitate the search for a partner. Help and assistance was often looked for at features of the sacred landscape, especially at wishing wells and trees, and at stone seats considered wishing chairs. Many a Christian shrine has been visited, and a praying stone turned in the intention to gain the patron saint's assistance in matters of love and marriage. A beautiful example for the latter is St Peakaun's Shrine in the Glen of Aherlow, County Tipperary with its holy well and sacred stones. Primarily valued for its healing virtues, the site took on matchmaking qualities during the first week in August, when making the pilgrimage was believed to bring a wedding within the following year.[3]

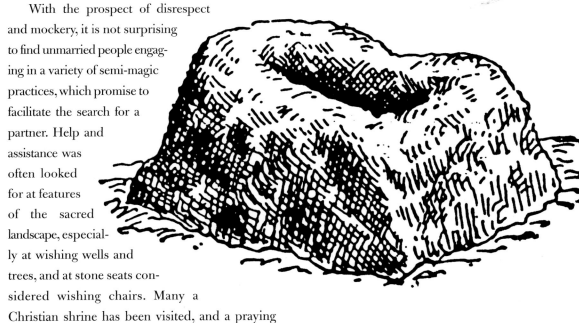

Cloch Daha, Ardmore, County Waterford

Each year, on Ash Wednesdays, the bachelors of Ardmore assembled at a bullaun stone, which was commonly known as Cloch Daha, the 'Good Stone' or the 'Stone of the Daghdha'. The men fixed a pole into the basin of the bullaun, and made the unmarried women of the village dance around the structure. Local authorities removed the stone at the end of the nineteenth century, but there are allegations that is was preserved in a private garden at least until the 1940s.[5]

Other wishing stones – usually sacred megaliths – were once exclusively venerated for their matchmaking and aphrodisiac qualities. In Furness, in County Kildare, for instance stands an impressive Bronze Age monolith, which is locally known as the Long Stone or as the *Fear Bréagach*, the False Man. Girls hoping to marry soon used to visit the granite pillar and hammer a pin into the hawthorn that was growing nearby. The tree was possibly a substitute, as we learn from other monoliths of weaker material in Central Europe, that nails and pins had to be hammered right into the stones as a prerequisite to release their magic.[4] The pin may just as well have been a present or reward for the stone, as both the fulfilment of certain preconditions and the deposition of an offering were customary when visiting sacred megaliths ceremonially.

**Proleek Dolmen,
County Louth**

The dolmen near the golf course is locally known as the 'Giant's Load'. Formerly a popular resort for people of either gender who wanted to find themselves a partner, it is now rather regarded as a general wishing stone which would grant any type of request. To evoke the magic power of the dolmen, it is necessary to throw a small pebble onto the capstone. If the pebble does not fall down, the applicant can assume that she or he will be married within a year, or alternatively that the wish will come true within the same period of time.[6]

Grey Stone, Corran, County Armagh

Local lore has it that the 'Grey Stone' on Corran Hill marks the burial place of the mad bull or bull god who tried to prevent St Patrick from spreading the new faith in south Armagh. Earlier popular tradition linked the pillar to the Donn Cuailnge, the dark bull from the Táin Bó Cuailnge. The association with the vigorous animal, and the conspicuous shape of the stone, have certainly led to the aphrodisiac connotation of the pillar, which became prominent among men in search of a wife. To make sure that any woman of his choice would not be able to refuse him, a man had to walk around the pillar three times. There were additional conditions involved but they were lost by the time the custom had been investigated for the first time in the 1930s.[7]

Holed Stones and the Pledge of Love

The tradition of sealing an agreement at specifically designated treaty stones builds on the principle belief that the stability and strength of the stone would lend confirmation to the spoken word; in addition, the stone would figure as an indestructible and irremovable witness to the contract.[8]

Throughout the Indo-European world, perforated stones were apparently the preferred type of treaty stones, where parties sealed agreements ranging from general bargains and deals to the promise of engagement and marriage by joining hands through the aperture. Especially popular – and usually firmly linked to the pledge of love and truth between young couples – were holed treaty stones in Norway and in those parts of Scotland which stood politically and culturally for considerable lengths of time under Scandinavian control.[9]

Odin's Stone, Stenness, Orkney Islands, Scotland
(this page)

The Bargaining Stone, Inis Cealtra, County Clare
(opposite page)

The early monastic settlement on the island in Lough Derg on the Shannon was a notable pilgrimage site, until Catholic authorities proscribed the pattern in the early decades of the nineteenth century. Prior to the intervention of the Church, the Bargaining Stone has been a popular meeting place to settle all kinds of contracts from marriage arrangements to the sale of land. The parties would shake hands through the hole to affirm the deal, trusting that a breach of the agreement would consequently result in great misfortunes for the transgressor. Fr MacNamara, in his booklet on the Holy Island, does not link the stone with bargains and deals. He refers to the Kissing Stone, where lovers 'pressed their lips to either end of the channel and vowed to love each other truly for evermore'.[10]

Probably the most famous example was Odin's Stone at Stenness, on the Orkney Islands. Norse Vikings, still pagan at that time, conquered the Orkneys in the late eighth century and introduced the cult of their chief deity Odin, together with the custom to seal contracts by giving the Promise of Odin. Initially a vow affirmed by joining hands through a massive ring of silver, which was kept especially for that purpose, the promise was later performed at perforated pillar stones of pre-Viking origin. At Stenness, the link to Odin survived the introduction of Christianity and the withdrawal of the Vikings in 1470. A report from 1784 tells of how young couples would meet on the first day of the year at Odin's Stone, where they would kneel and pray to Odin to enable them to be good partners; then, they would clasp hands through the perforation to confirm their commitments. The promise given at Odin's Stone was considered sacred, and reportedly very popular. Unfortunately, the steady stream of visitors annoyed a local farmer and he destroyed the stone in 1814 or 1815.

The Love Stone of Doagh, County Antrim

The beautiful whinstone pillar stands about 1 mile from the village of Doagh, and seems to be of Bronze Age origin. Traditionally called the Hole Stone, it is recently and more affectionately dubbed the Love Stone; local couples promising each other eternal love would join hands through the hole in the hope of fastening their bond and securing for themselves a happy marriage. As the stone is believed not to accept a male hand, it would always be the girl who has to pass her hand through the aperture. A notice at the site informs that conventions at the Hole Stone can be traced back to about 1830. Initially, lovers would have resorted to the stone to confirm their intention to marry and had apparently understood the stone as a symbol for an engagement ring. After a decline of almost half a century, the practice has been revived in modern times.[11]

Like their counterparts in Norway and Scotland, the perforated contract stones of Ireland were primarily resorted to in matters of love and marriage. The stones, as such, seem to belong to different periods from the Bronze Age to early Christian times; characteristically, they are not directly associated with saints, and there are no references of any specific Christian performances attached to them. The origin of their implication in marriage customs is unknown. As they occur often in areas of Viking or Scottish influence, it is, however, reasonable to suggest that the idea to substitute a holed stone for an engagement ring is based on Scandinavian traditions.

An Irish variant of the Promise of Odin was the Teltown Marriage, which belonged until about 1700 to the annual festival of Teltown in County Meath. Couples joining hands through the Marriage Hollow which was, in fact, a hole in a wooden gate, would have pledged themselves to each other for the duration of one year.[12]

A magnificent example of a holed treaty stone in Ireland is the Marriage Stone or *Cloch na nGeallúna*, the Promising Stone, on Cape Clear in County Cork. It is the northern-most member of the Pillars of Comolán or *Galláin an Chomaláin*, a Bronze Age stone alignment near the north western point of Cape Clear. Island tradition recalls that young couples used to shake hands through the aperture in the pillar to confirm their commitment to each other, trusting that through the power of the stone their promise would never be broken.[13]

Sacred Stones and Progeny

Especially in rural societies, a childless marriage is considered an economic and social tragedy. For the poor, children mean contributors to the household and providers for the old age; for the landed class, they are vital to guarantee that property and land remains in the family. In ancient Ireland progeny was of such importance that the Brehon Laws forbade impotent men to marry; had one of the partners proved sterile only after the marriage, this would have been regarded a reason for a 'blameless' divorce. During the eighteenth century, trial marriages in Counties Antrim, Derry and Fermanagh would prove if the couple could procreate. Well into the twentieth century in Ireland, as in most part of Europe, sterility was still regarded a disgrace.[14]

With the ancient powerful link of the
earth goddess and her later manifestation
to fecundity and procreation, it does not
come as a surprise to find remnants of her
cult surviving into fairly recent fertility-
promoting rituals and ceremonies.

In the western half of Ireland especially,
dolmens were once highly valued among
women wishing to have a child. In order
to facilitate conception, they would have
slept on the capstones of the monuments.
Dolmens are frequently erected with the
entrance facing the rising sun, and there
are indications that they stood anciently
in connection with the sun goddess Grian.
Popular lore would later link dolmens to
Gráinne and Diarmaid, the fugitive couple
running from Fionn mac Cumhaill, and
point them out as beds built by the lovers
during their flight.[16]

In Brittany, dolmens with similar
pregnancy-promoting qualities were popularly known as 'hot stones'. Until the early
twentieth century, girls and women wishing to get married or have children rubbed
their naked body to the stones, or brought
their partners to spend the night with them
at the monuments.[17]

Christian tradition adopted a belief in
the curative and fertilising virtues of a night

spent in a divine bed, and transferred it to the 'beds' of saints. Among the most visited is Patrick's Bed on the summit of Croagh Patrick, County Mayo. Today, it is customary for pilgrims to lie down on the bed; into the early nineteenth century, only those who desired children would have come to the bed to spend a night on it.

The custom to sleep on sacred stone beds for their fertilising potential has long been abolished. When present-day women seek the assistance of stones related to the goddess, they would resort to carvings of Sheela-na-Gigs.

This term – often said to derive from the name *Síle na gCíoch* or Síle of the Paps – is very likely to be an invention of nineteenth-century antiquarians. It has nevertheless become the most common name for carvings of naked female figures that emphasise the genital area. About 100 Sheelas have been identified in Ireland; smaller numbers occur in England, Scotland, France and Spain.

There is controversy about their origin, and the initial purpose of the carvings. Today, experts prefer theories of a continental provenence, and suggest that the idea stems from the anti-feminist propaganda of the medieval Church. Introduced to Ireland, the native tradition would have

Sheela-na-Gig, the goddess of fertility; Ballyvourney (opposite page) **and Castlemagner, County Cork** (left)

St Gobnait's Shrine at Ballyvourney is a highly venerated place of pilgrimage and hundreds flock to the place around the pattern day on 11 February. Pious visitors would often describe the little carving over the window of St Gobnait's Abbey as an image of the patron saint, though it has been clearly identified as a Sheela-na-Gig. As part of the observances at Ballyvourney, women wishing to conceive would climb up to rub the genital area of the Sheela. For the same purpose women would touch the withered carving of a Sheela on St Adamnán's Cross, one of the sacred gatepost stones at the Hill of Tara.

The carving on the entrance to the healing well at Castlemagner is locally believed to represent a Sheela-na-Gig. Women hoping to become pregnant or seeking a cure for female complaints, use a pebble to mark the signs of the cross on hands, forehead and above the belly of the carving; the rubbings are carefully saved and taken with water from the well. A visit during the month of May is considered particularly effective.

**Toberaraght or
St Attracta's Well,
Monasteraden, County Sligo**

*The fifth-century saint Attracta
was a highly renowned miracle
worker and healer. Her well
outside Monasteraden, County
Sligo, is reputed to have a cure
for various diseases, and is considered particularly helpful with
regards to warts and rickets. The
well is surrounded by a low wall,
which has several rounded
stones cemented to its top.
People visiting the site to restore
their health would initially have
handled these stones; women
seeking their assistance with
regards to conception and
childbirth took them home for a
limited period of time. The
custom was almost forgotten
when modern traditions began
to recall the fertility aspect
of the 'serpent eggs'; two
unattached speckled pebbles
have since appeared on the
wall, ready to be applied in
the old ways.*[18]

associated the iconography of the Sheela-na-Gig with their own ancient perception of a mother goddess and adopted her accordingly. Maureen Concannon, in the most recent study of Sheela-na-Gigs, outlines the changing perceptions of the carvings, beginning with the earth mother and her link to fertility, to the deity of sovereignty and her protective functions, and to the spiritual significance for present-day women.[19]

At several holy wells, dedicated to female saints of the early Celtic Church, rounded altar stones would locally be known as 'serpent eggs'. These 'eggs' are believed to possess fertilising virtues and women desiring to become pregnant would turn the stones in order to evoke their inhibiting power. After a decline in the practice from the second half of the twentieth century, some 'serpent eggs' experience a recent revival.

Birth Stones to Assist in Labour

St Colmcille's biographer relates that while carrying out his missionary work on Tory Island in County Donegal, the saint used a stone for a pillow to rest on. Before he left the island, he blessed the stone, which thereafter 'works many miracles and marvels, and water wherein it is steeped doth succour women in labour forthwith, of little so ever they may drink hereof'. In installing a stone that would particularly facilitate childbirth, Colmcille might have looked back at the tradition of his own birth on a designated birth stone his mother Eithne had been directed to. This stone, an impressive cup-marked flag, is still preserved in Colmcille's birthplace near Gartan in County Donegal.[20]

The most conventional birth stones in nineteenth- and twentieth-century Ireland were rounded healing stones and perforated pillars. We have already seen that several pillar stones with small circular perforations were employed to give the Promise of Odin, that is to pledge love and fidelity. More commonly, such stones were highly revered for their curative properties, primarily, though not exclusively, in connection with childbirth and specific female problems. In contrast to holed treaty stones, birth stones would characteristically appear near early monastic settlements, and prayers would be prerequisites to release their power. The stones themselves seem to be early Christian cross-inscribed pillars; the original function of the perforations has been subject to various theories but remains obscure; it could

**St Ciarán's Stone,
Inishmore, County Galway**

have been a continuation or development from the likewise uncertain Bronze Age cult of cutting holes into monoliths.

Accounts regarding Cloch na Peacaib at Kilquhone in County Cork, or St Ciaran's Stone on Inishmore in County Galway show that using holed pillars in order to ensure a favourable delivery, women nearing their confinement would have drawn a piece of cloth through the hole, and kept the fabric on them while giving birth.[21]

Rounded birth stones were regularly 'borrowed' shortly before women went into labour, and kept at home until after the child was born. Usually, those stones were also renowned for their general healing virtues; they occur almost exclusively at early monastic sites, and are firmly linked to the local patron saint.

Likewise in a clear Christian context stand several natural rock cavities, which were especially valued by pregnant women. In Our Lady's Bed on Inishmore in Lough Gill, County Sligo, and in St Kevin's Bed in Glendalough County Wicklow, expectant mothers used to lie and pray that they might not die in labour.

Leac na Cumha, Gartan, County Donegal

St Colmcille was born in the Gartan area in about 521 AD, and a flagstone – Leac na Cumha – is reputed to mark the spot. His biographers relate that shortly before his mother Eithne came down, angels advised her to get a particular birth stone, a flag she would find floating on Gartan Lake. She duly came with her kinsmen to carry the stone home, but on the journey back her waters broke, transforming the ground into fine white clay. Until today only Eithne's folk can lift the clay, which is famous for its protecting powers and for the virtue of relieving the pains of labour.[22]

According to local tradition, Colmcille returned to his birth stone before he had to leave Ireland, and spent his last night in the country sleeping on the cup-marked flag. Since then, the birth stone became known as Leac na Cumha, or the Flagstone of Loneliness, and is trusted to ease heartache and sorrow, especially the pain of homesickness, in those who spend a night on the stone as Colmcille did.

Holed Stone, Inishmurray, County Sligo

One of the standing stones inside the old monastic enclosure on Inishmurray bears two curious perforations. They both commence on the wide western face with holes just large enough to take a thumb, and emerge on the small faces of the stone with larger apertures that can easily hold the fingers. It was customary for the women of the island to kneel in front of this stone, with the thumbs in the small holes, and the fingers in the openings to the sides, while praying for conception and later for a favourable confinement. Local tradition insists that owing to the holed stone not a single island woman has ever died in childbirth.[23]

Caipín Ólainn (St Ólann's Cap), Aghabulloge, County Cork

Celebrated for its healing virtues as well as for its ability to return home on its own account was St Ólann's Cap, a quartzite that sat on top of an Ogham-inscribed pillar stone in the old cemetery of Aghabulloge. It was credited with the power to cure headaches if the suffering person walked three times around the ruined church while carrying the Cap on the head. Women would regularly have borrowed the stone to avail of its curative properties for female ailments or to relieve the pains of labour. Quartz, with its association to the moon and to the mother goddess, was held in high regard since Neolithic times. Christianity interpreted the crystalline stone as a symbol of purity and linked it to the Virgin Mary. Nevertheless, in the nineteenth century, the Catholic clergy denounced the use of the Cap and removed it from Aghabulloge. Locals had quickly replaced Ólann's Cap by a similar quartzite, which inherited the healing virtues of its predecessor; unfortunately, since being cemented to the pillar, it can no longer be used in the traditional manner.[24]

Stones of Healing

This stone was called in Irish, Cloch Ruadh, *and it was of a tapering shape, like a golden apple. It was used to bear that stone about to houses, where infirm persons were in danger of death, and especially was it in request for women in cases of difficult parturition.*

John O'Hanlon, *Life of St Colmcille* (1875)

The Plague Stone and the Three Monks, Tomfinlough, County Clare

An enchanting tale of trust in the healing power of a saint stems from east Clare. Saint Luctigern, the founder of Tomfinlough Abbey, worked the field with three monks when a young woman afflicted with the Plague approached them. Luctigern made the sign of the cross over the swellings on the woman's forehead, took them off and flung them against the wall, thus restoring the woman's health. One of the monks immediately knelt down and praised God upon this miracle, the second monk was not sure what to think of it, while the third did not believe at all and started to mock. The saint did not say a word, but carved the images of the monks in stones and fixed them to the wall. The next morning the face of the monk who did not believe had entirely withered away; the sceptical monk was only half-recognisable, while the face of the believer remains unchanged to this day. A visit to the stone heads and the Plague Stone, the latter featuring the petrified swellings, is still part of the pilgrimage to Tomfinlough. The carvings were initially trusted to keep epidemics out of the parish; with the Plague no longer a threat, visitors would now touch the stones in order to obtain a cure for all types of ailments.[1]

Depending on their respective beliefs and natural resources, cultures around the world have developed a variety of magic and religious healing practices. In Ireland, as in most parts of Europe, help was and indeed is often sought at particular wells, which were reputed to possess curative qualities; to a smaller, but still significant degree, patients hoped to obtain a cure with the support of healing stones.

We get a good picture of the use and significance of healing stones from the nineteenth century onwards, but the practice is undoubtedly much older. Ancient magical traits survived in the procedures

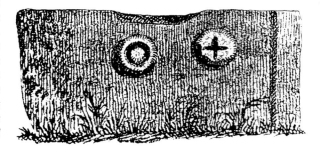

that are required to release the power of healing stones, and in the necessity to connect physically with the healing stone or at least with an object that has previously been applied to it. This precondition – just as the notion that the power and essence of the saint who had once touched or blessed the stone would remain

with it forever – builds on the concept of contagious magic, the belief that things that had once been in contact remain spiritually connected.[2]

Today, healing stones are almost invariably embedded in Christian traditions; we find them usually near holy wells or early ecclesiastic sites, named after the respective patron saints who have traditionally bestowed them with their healing virtues and left instructions on their proper and effective use. Prayers and sometimes a preparatory fast are common parts of a ceremonial visit to healing stones, and pilgrims trusting in the power of saints and their sacred stones would attribute a successful cure to a miracle rather than to an act of magic.

Healing stones are a common feature in all parts of the country, too numerous to even contemplate a complete list of them. Together with healing wells, curative stones remained popular into the early decades of the twentieth century, and many of them still attract considerable numbers of patients. Today, people would often resort to them in addition to a visit to a doctor, or in cases when conventional medicine has no help to offer.

Crawling Under the Healing Stones

Particularly for the cure of backaches and rheumatism, a patient would often have to squeeze through cleft rocks, or to crawl under a rock or through the aperture of a stone. In a spiritual sense, this practice could be considered a symbolic rebirth or regeneration without the old ailments, though the procedure may well have developed with the idea of drawing strength from the material, or more practically, to literally rub off pains and aches. Similar observances are carried out abroad; in India they are part of rites to regenerate spiritually; on the Continent, in Scotland and in England, they are performed for healing purposes.

A popular type of stone for this kind of healing were holed pillars from the megalithic period; those exemplars with apertures large enough for people to crawl through are probably those so-called 'port-hole stones', which were sometimes used to close the chambers of early Bronze Age tombs; the holes would have been exits for the souls or openings for offerings to the dead. Popular tradition associates the monuments often with mythic heroes, and it is possible that the idea to 'draw strength' from the stone stems from the legendary link. Into the nineteenth century, parents passed their children through such holes to prevent or cure infant diseases, but the custom has long since come to an end. Stones with Christian associations on the other hand, be they natural boulders or man-made structures, still enjoy considerable popularity.

St Declan's Stone Boat, Ardmore, County Waterford

The pilgrimage to Ardmore is traditionally carried out on 24 July, and involves stations at the ruined church, at the holy well, and at St Declan's Stone. In 1841, Mr and Mrs Hall describe the ritual: 'After praying their devotions at the grave, the people crowd to the Holystone, and having gone on their bare knees several times round it, creep under it, lying flat on the belly. The painful contortions of some of these poor people it is distressing to witness, as they force themselves, through the narrow passage'. It was firmly believed that crawling under the stone would cure backache and rheumatism, given that the patient had nothing borrowed or stolen on her or him. Moreover, anyone who had committed a mortal sin would not be able to pass under the stone. Westropp relates the story of an unfortunate woman who got stuck under the boulder and had to be pulled out by her feet. It was commonly reckoned that the stone had lowered itself and caught her for whatever sin she had committed.[3]

Cloch Liath (Grey Stone) or Cloch Bhreac (Speckled Stone), Tobernaveen, County Sligo (above)

The Cloch Liath stands in the vicinity of the Carrowmore megalithic cemetery, and could well have been a port-hole stone to a grave chamber. Tradition, however, insists that it was set up to mark the old meeting point of three parishes. Throughout the nineteenth century, mothers passed weak or sick children through the hole to restore them to health and strength. Today, nearby Tobar na bhFian has flooded the surrounding area and the stone is hardly accessible.[4]

St Ronan's Mass Table, Kilronan, County Roscommon (left)

St Lassair's Holy Well lies in a small garden at the shore of Lough Mealy or Meelagh and is named after the daughter of the local saint, Ronan. A bullaun on the bank of the small stream which flows from the well is popularly known as the holy Font of St Ronan or as the Cleansing Stone, and visitors to the well would wash their face, hands and feet in its water as part of the pilgrimage. Patients suffering from backache would then proceed to St Ronan's Altar, a flagstone raised c 2 feet above the ground, and crawl under it. The task is difficult – even for people in good physical shape – but considered very effective and pilgrimages to St Ronan's are still popular.[5]

Rounded Healing Stones

A very interesting feature at early monastic sites and holy wells in their neighbourhood are – particularly in the west of Ireland – rounded, egg-shaped stones, which usually rest on simple *leachta* or dry-stone altars, in bullauns or occasionally on unadorned slabs or flagstones.

The oval shape of the stones had led to speculations on their pre-Christian significance with regards to fertility symbolism or the cult of the human head. The Irish antiquarian and architect, George Petrie, on the other hand, suggested that early missionaries carried consecrated stones on their journey, and placed them on altars when celebrating Mass. He refers to a passage in the Book of Lecan regarding St Aire, 'who left no heirs but mass stones' when he died in 737 AD.[6]

Folklore, based on the respective passages in the biographies of saints, believes that early missionaries left rounded stones as tokens to the converted communities before moving on to spread the faith elsewhere. The stones preserved the essence of the saint and, following the saint's instructions on their proper use, enabled the community to communicate with the divine. They can serve as praying, healing, wishing or cursing stones, and visitors would touch them or turn them to emphasise their request. The healing stones among them are still resorted to in many places; any movement involved in their ritual use has to be carried out in the beneficial clockwise direction.

**The Homing Stones of
Caher Island, County Mayo**
(left and opposite page)

*In 1900, the Irish writer T.W.
Rolleston visited Caher Island.
Locals told him that not long
ago, 'one visitor attempted to
remove a large piece of pumice
stone, about the size of a foot-
ball, which lies on one of the
leachta, but an accident which
happened to his boat on the
homeward journey convinced
him that he was transgressing
a sacred prohibition, and he
returned and replaced the stone'.
The stone in question lies on the
altar to the east of the ruined
Teampull na Naomh or Teampull
Phadraig. In recent times the
stone had twice disappeared,
only to reappear soon afterwards on Caher Island. A similar
story is occasionally told of the
quartzite stone, which rests on
an altar on the small hillock
near the ruined church, but
people from the neighbouring
islands insist that the actual
homing stone is the large
pumice pebble.*[7]

Since rounded stones are rather small, it was easy to comply with the condition to connect physically, even for patients too sick or too feeble to travel. If required, immobile patients could borrow a healing stone from the sacred site. Out of respect for the sanctity of the stones, and in the firm belief that it is unlucky to steal them or keep them longer than necessary, they were for centuries duly returned after use. The borrowing and returning of healing stones has certainly been the basis for the once wide-spread tales of 'homing stones', which would always transport themselves miraculously back to their original position, no matter how far they had been removed.[8]

Occasionally rounded stones were also used to cure animals. Among the most beautiful examples are St Patrick's Stones in Killerry, County Sligo. St Patrick, it is told, was not allowed to cross the ford at Sligo and had to ride around Lough Gill instead. On the rough ground, his horse hurt the sinew of

St Patrick's Stones, Killerry, County Sligo

The stones at Killerry are famous for effectively healing pains and injuries. A 1913 description of the procedure known as 'lifting a strain thread' as follows: 'A friend of the sufferer goes to Killerry and brings a piece of thread, which should in strictness be of unbleached linen, though this condition is not always adhered to. On arrival at the place the thread is wrapped round the peg-like stone mentioned above; the round stones are then turned separately while a prayer is said; afterward the thread left by some former visitor is taken up, brought to the patient, and bound round the affected part; the cure soon follows'. The healing ritual is still performed in the same way. Patients well enough to travel to Killerry themselves would additionally apply the stones to the aching part of their body at some stage of the ritual.[9]

St Conall's Healing Stones, Bruckless, County Donegal
(left and below)

Part of a pilgrimage to St Conall's Holy Well is a visit to the nearby cairn, called An Altóir. When Wood-Martin described the cairn in 1902, he noted a dumb-bell shaped stone, which was supposed to cure all types of ailments. If required, the stone was brought to a patient's house and kept there until the cure had worked; it had once even been sent to America to heal a native of this part of Donegal. Sadly, the healing stone eventually disappeared in the 1960s. St Conall's shrine, however, has not lost its curative virtues, and a notice at the cairn instructs pilgrims to put the wrist of the right arm into the notch of an upright stone on the Altóir, and three fingers of the left hand into the perforation of another stone beside it. Remaining in this position, some prescribed prayers are said before the pilgrim formulates the request for healing or any other wish.[10]

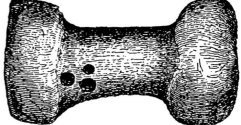

his foot. The saint picked seven stones and used them successfully to heal the horse; he blessed the stones, leaving the curative power for people and animals on them forever. As late as 1841, another healing stone for animals was kept at Curraghmore House, County Waterford. Known as the 'Murrain Stone', it has been frequently borrowed by local farmers to cure murrain in cattle. For that purpose, they placed the stone in water, and drove the cattle through it.[11]

The Curative Power of Stone Beds

The principle of incubation, that is, spiritual transformation and regeneration through sleep, predates Christianity and was often practiced on or near the tombs of important mystical or historical characters. Remnants of the custom had long survived in the form of spending a night on particular Neolithic dolmens in order to facilitate conception. The Christian doctrine adapted the idea of the special virtues that rest in the grave of significant people and installed shrines for saints and relics.

The earliest shrines would have been stone slabs marking the burial place of a saint. In Ireland, these graves became popularly known as a saint's *leaba* or bed, a term which also denotes the traditional sleeping or resting places of saints in natural rock cavities or on flagstones in oratories and cells. Whether grave or place for the night, the beds of saints are ascribed healing virtues for a variety of ailments and diseases, particularly for epileptic fits and problems regarding conception and confinement. Earlier sources indicate that patients actually had to spend one or more nights on the stony beds; more recently, it is generally considered sufficient to lie in the beds for a short while, turning several times.[12]

From the late twelfth century, altar tombs appear as a characteristic feature of Gothic church architecture. They combined in themselves the concepts of the stone altars of the early Celtic Church and the traditional veneration of the graves or beds of saints, and attracted popular devotion and lore in very much the same way as those earlier monuments. Altar tombs would usually carry carved images of the interred person, or of apostles or saints; people wishing to avail of the curative virtues of the monuments would touch or kiss the figures, especially their heads; sleeping on the tombs, however, was apparently not customary.

**St Patrick's Bed,
Caher Island, County Mayo**

*Caher Island is traditionally
associated with St Patrick.
A cross-inscribed slab below
the eastern wall of the ruined
church is pointed out as the
bed on which the saint slept
during his stay on the island.
Others reckon that it might
mark the grave of Patrick's
charioteer who allegedly died
on Caher. The bed has the
reputation for curing epilepsy
in any patient who would
sleep on it.[13]*

St Conall's Bed, Bruckless, County Donegal

A flat stone beyond the cairn at St Conall's shrine is alternatively known as St Conall's Bed or St Conall's Table. Until the early decades of the twentieth century, visitors spent a night on the rock to obtain a cure. Today it is considered sufficient to stretch out on the bed and turn three times.[14]

Altar Slab, Tobar na Mult, Ardfert, County Kerry

Tobar na Mult, or the Wethers' Well, still attracts numerous pilgrims and is believed to offer a cure for different health problems, particularly rheumatism. As part of the prescribed 'rounds' at the well, visitors touch or kiss the faces of the carved figures on the slab that forms the front of the altar. The images traditionally represent the patron saints of the little shrine, namely St Ite who is buried on the site, St Erc who preached here, and St Brendan, who was baptised by St Erc with the waters of the well. The slab was part of a late medieval altar tomb, and has been used for serving Mass during Penal Times. It figures prominently in local lore, and is supposed to be irremovable, with numerous stories referring to failed attempts to carry it away.[15]

Bullauns and Imprint Stones

Bullaun stones are boulders with basins of natural or artificial origin; throughout Ireland we find them in the vicinity of early Christian monastic settlements, but their origin and initial purpose remain obscure. Recent historical and archaeological reports tend to date them to the transitional period between the Iron Age and early Christianity, and reckon that they might have been introduced by the Roman world as grinding stones for new types of cereals; earlier studies preferred to link bullaun stones with either pagan or early Christian religious traditions.

Folklore has found its own distinct interpretations: bullaun stones with basins of natural origin are traditionally taken as imprint stones bearing the marks of a saint's body, head or limbs; consequently ascribed healing properties, patients would place the corresponding part of the body into the basins. Artificially created basin stones, on the other hand, are popularly interpreted as baptism fonts from the early Celtic Church, or as holy water stoops if they occur beside the entrances to old churches. In the twelfth century, Giraldus Cambrensis gave his own fanciful account of the function of bullauns. 'In the South of Munster near Cork there is a certain island which has within it a church of St Michael, revered for its true holiness from ancient times. There is a certain stone there outside of, but almost touching, the door of the church on the right-hand side. In a hollow of the upper part of this stone there is found every morning through the merits of the saints of the place as much wine as is necessary for the celebrations of as many Masses as there are priests to say Mass on that day there.'[16]

Several bullaun stones contain rounded stones in their depressions, which would have been turned for working a curse or a cure, or for emphasising a prayer or a wish. Others bear water and it is commonly understood that the water would never evaporate, not even during long periods without rain. They form the perfect combination of a healing well and stone; popularly known as wart stones, they are primarily responsible for warts and other skin disorders.[17]

The Deer Stone, Glendalough, County Wicklow

To obtain a cure at the Deer Stone, pilgrims were supposed to visit on a Sunday, Tuesday and Thursday of the same week, and to circumvent the stone seven times on bare knees on each visit. The name of the stone recalls a legend of the local patron saint, Kevin. Upon his prayers, a deer came regularly to the bullaun and left her milk in the hollow to feed an infant whose mother had died in childbirth.[18]

Doughnambraher Font, Killeen, County Clare

Doughnambraher Font or the Friar's Vat stands in a field near the remains of an old burial ground for unbaptised children. Tradition has it that the founder of a former church or abbey at Killeen lies buried under the stone, but the history of the monastic settlement is lost. The font is locally known as a wart stone, and it is believed that the cure lies in the seven rounded stones which rest in its water-filled cavity. To make warts disappear, they should be rubbed with the stones. Coins left in the basin or under the stone indicate that people still trust in its virtues.[19]

**St Brigid's Shrine,
Faughart, County Louth**
(right and opposite page)

*St Brigid was, according
to her biographers, born in
about 454, near Faughart, a
few miles from her modern
shrine. The shrine was
established in 1934, and the
first Sunday in July installed
as the date for the annual
pilgrimage. The stations in the
upper section of the shrine take
in St Brigid's Fountain and
Stream; the lower part
features a variety of highly
venerated healing stones.*

*Two bullaun stones marked by
Brigid's tears and eyes are
renowned for easing eye
problems. Another stone bears
the marks of the saint's knees,
and pilgrims would kneel in the
impressions to cure pains of the
limbs. The headstone, built
into a low wall, is regarded as
particularly effective in
relieving headaches.*[20]

Stones of Spiritual Transformation

'The stone [i.e. St John's Stone at Drumcullen, County Offaly] is a large virgin rock, five feet high and eight or nine feet long. The deep crevices in it, and the ground about it, are strewn with the most varied objects, rosary beads, little devotional images and cards, buttons of all kinds down to the linen variety, clasps, brooches, pipe bowls, even money. The objects were accounted for by a little girl of the locality. "If you say a prayer at the rock and leave something there, you leave your sins behind you."'

Olive Purser, *JRSAI 48* (1919)[1]

Pilgrimage in Stone

Visits to sacred places can be enormous spiritual experiences, which transform and raise consciousness, bring religious inspiration and encourage the process of healing. In their present form, communal pilgrimages at fixed dates are a legacy of the early Celtic Church, though the practice to gather ceremonially at sacred wells, around stones and ancient stone monuments and on hilltops, has been a significant aspect of social and religious life long before Christianity arrived in the country.

The main ceremonial assembly dates of pagan Ireland were the days that divided the year into four seasonal quarters, with the festivals traditionally starting at sunset on the day before the actual feast.

**Labyrinth Stone,
Hollywood, County Wicklow**

The decorated granite boulder was discovered near the old pilgrimage route to St Kevin's monastery at Glendalough, and was probably a spiritual or practical signpost for early pilgrims. The symbol of the labyrinth was popular in early Christian Europe and usually understood as a representation of the path that leads from the outer world to the inner consciousness, and to God. The motif itself is certainly earlier, and seems to be related to the ancient spirals and concentric circles which stood for the cycle of life, death and recreation.[2]

Imbolc or Oimelg was held around 1 February. The meaning of both terms is uncertain but we know that the feast marked the beginning of springtime and celebrated the start of tilling and the birth of livestock. Imbolc was the festival of the Celtic goddess Brigid, daughter of the Daghdha and a mother goddess associated with fertility and healing, with fire, sun and water. Many traits of the goddess survived her transformation into her namesake saint, and healing wells and stones now dedicated to St Brigid are still popular sites of pilgrimages. Bealtaine, around 1 May, was regarded as the beginning of summer and the start of the grassing season. The festival was inseparably connected with sacred fires, and cattle were driven through them for protection. The name Bealtaine means probably 'Fire of Bel', and it is possible that the customary May Day fires were initially lit in honour of the god Bel or Belenus. The largest Bealtaine assemblies in ancient Ireland were held on the Hill of Uisneach, traditionally the site where for the first time ever a ceremonial fire was set alight in the country. According to medieval literature, it is also the day when the Celts first arrived in Ireland.

The harvest festival of Lughnasa at the start of autumn recalls the Celtic deity and hero Lugh Lámhfhada; the feast has survived into modern times and is still celebrated under various names around the beginning of August. Samhain, literally the 'end of the summer', was the festival of the disappearing sun and the start of the Celtic new year. It occurred around 1 November and had strong associations with death and the otherworld.[3]

Leac na Teine, Inishmurray, County Sligo

Leac na Teine, or the Stone of the Fire on Inishmurray in County Sligo seems to be a remnant of an ancient fire cult. In 1836, O'Donovan reports that some islanders hold the tradition of a perpetual fire being formerly kept on the flagstone for the use of the people of Inishmurray. Others told him that if all the fires went out on Inishmurray, a sod of turf or a piece of wood applied to the cold flag would ignite immediately. The latter tale in particular is still popular today; island lore preserves the memory of a foreign visitor to Inishmurray who profaned the remarkable flagstone by urinating on it. At once, a fire flared up to consume the offender. Fragments of cremated human bones were long kept in a niche of the building and pointed out as the unfortunate man's remains.[4]

When Christianity began to spread, the seasonal assembly sites and other places of earlier spiritual significance were gradually transformed into Christian shrines, usually by the blessing of an early missionary or saint. Pagan rituals and observations were adapted to the new faith and incorporated into the canon of the Celtic Church, and communal conventions at sacred places became known as pilgrimages.

The set date for communal pilgrimages was usually the feast day of the local patron saint. The common term pattern for a pilgrimage derives from the Irish word *pátrún* for patron saint. Patterns were initially lively festivals with religious devotion, music and dancing, courting and sometimes 'faction-fighting' among the participants. Church reforms in medieval times had begun to shift the focus of pilgrimages towards penance and endurance, and by the twelfth century, the new concept had reached Ireland and co-existed with the earlier patterns. Irrespective of the disapproval by the established Churches and the temporary prohibition of the traditional pilgrimages, they survived well into the nineteenth century. It was only then that the re-organised Catholic Church successfully removed the festival-like and entertaining elements from the old pattern and place religious devotion into the centre of pilgrimage. In this modernised form, patterns are still alive today.

A pilgrimage is a ritual walk or a sacred journey – also known as *turas* – which takes place at several sacred places like old churches, wells, trees or stones. Those features are the stations of the pilgrimage, the places where pilgrims stop to pray and perform the prescribed rituals. The *turas* is a circular walk, leading clockwise from station to station, and clockwise again around the individual station markers.

One of the oldest pilgrimages of Christian Ireland is *An Turas Cholmcille*, St Colmcille's Station or Journey at Glencolumbcille, County Donegal, which begins ideally at midnight preceding the saint's feast day on 9 June. The pilgrimage follows a three-mile route through the valley, and takes three to four hours to complete. Historians date its origin to the eighth or ninth century, but oral tradition claims that Colmcille himself initiated the pilgrimage in the first half of the sixth century, and left *lec nime*, the 'stone slabs of Heaven', to mark the fifteen praying stations for the devotees.

Throughout the country, most of the ancient pilgrimage sites have at least one sacred stone as a

The Boheh Stone (opposite page) **and Croagh Patrick** (left; seen from Caher Island)**, County Mayo**

The Boheh Stone stands on one of the old pilgrimage routes to Croagh Patrick, about 5 miles from the mountain. It has long been 'Christianised' and is popularly known as St Patrick's Chair. From 1987, the Westport historian, Gerry Bracken, has surveyed and investigated a possible relation between the Boheh Stone and Croagh Patrick – and came to a striking result. To the observer looking from the stone towards the mountain on or about 18 April and 24 August, the setting sun appears to sit on top of the mountain before it seems to roll down along the northern slope.[5]

Croagh Patrick is certainly among the earliest sacred sites in the country. The mountain was linked to Lughnasa, to the Crom Dubh and the Caoranach, before St Patrick took over. One indication of its significance in pre-Christian times is the decorated stone in Boheh, dated to the late Stone Age or early Bronze Age and aligned with Croagh Patrick.

**Stations of the pilgrimage
at Glencolumbcille,
County Donegal**

St Colmcille's Bed (right)

*A stone slab known as
St Colmcille's Bed is part of a
station called The Chapel.
Pilgrims bless themselves with
a small stone from the alcove
above St Colmcille's Bed, and
pass it around the waist from
left to right. They then lie on the
stone bed and turn three times
in a clockwise direction. Clay
scooped from under the bed
has a cure for headaches, and
is also said to protect against
drowning, fire and lightning.*

St Colmcille's Well (right)

*Before they climb from
St Colmcille's Bed to the
holy well on the highest point
of the turas, visitors pick up
three stones. Later, when
walking three times around the
well, they emphasise the
completion of each round by
placing one of these stones
on the massive cairn that
has already built up.*

station marker. Glencolumbcille is a magnificent example of a pilgrimage focusing on sacred stones. The majority of the slabs are pillar stones, decorated with geometric patterns or cross motifs, but there are also unmodified boulders, flagstones and cairns. We would often find cairns at sacred places, particularly near holy wells, and built by pilgrims who wanted to leave behind a token of their presence. In those places it is customary to add a stone at the completion of a station; sometimes visitors are asked to carry this stone from another place along the *turas*, while elsewhere pilgrims take it from the bottom of the cairn and add it to the top.[6]

Áit na nGlún

A flag, initially topped by two rounded stones, is part of the station at Áit na nGlún, or the Place of the Knees. Pilgrims bless themselves with the first stone and pass it three times around their bodies in a clockwise direction; the ritual is repeated with the second stone. The stones are supposed to heal ailments of any part of the body touched by them. Recently, one of the healing stones has disappeared and locals fear it is now in a private collection.

Colmcille's Stone Boat

Beside a small stream on the track from St Colmcille's Bed down to the valley lies Colmcille's Boat, which once, according to legend, carried the saint across the waters. The boat is not an official station of the pilgrimage at Glencolumbcille, but pilgrims nevertheless stop to say a prayer and wash their feet with the water that gathers on the stone.

Wishing Stones and Lucky Talismans

Occasionally, people would refer to particular healing or cursing stones as wishing stones. A fervent prayer for a cure from ills and ailments or for the punishment of an offence is undoubtedly a wish or a request for divine assistance. Moreover, we can assume that certain sacred stones were generally credited with the power to fulfil any type of request. Other stones, however, are primarily prized for transforming spiritually, for bringing luck and success. Such explicit wishing stones and lucky talismans have neither links to cure nor curse, but are instead responsible for a variety of other requests that require supernatural support, covering a wide range from partnership and family, to school and business, to pastimes and sports.

There are fine examples of stone talismans of mermaids in medieval churches. The earliest documentation of reverence paid to a lucky idol – the Lucky Stone in Dublin – relates also to the medieval period. Lucky idols and wishing stones are customarily touched, rubbed or kissed to avail of their indwelling virtues. Typical is the absence of prayer or other Christian observations, even if the respective stone appears today in a purely Christian environment. Not even a request made to the granite cross which reputedly marks the burial place of St Kevin in Glendalough requires a prayer. Instead, an applicant has to fulfil an almost impossible task: to join fingers around the shaft of the cross while standing with the back to it. Difficult or daring tasks are often essential parts of the wishing ritual; likewise, it is also taboo to reveal the wish to anybody else.

The Lucky Stone, St Audoen's Church, Dublin

St Audoen's, built in the twelfth century, is dedicated to the Norman saint Ouen. The Lucky Stone came perhaps from an older church on this site, and seems to be an early Christian grave slab. In 1309, the first Lord Major of Dublin set the stone up beside a water trough near the church, and those who passed would touch or kiss the stone for good fortune, prosperity, or a safe journey.

The Lucky stone was removed in 1826 by the clergy, only to be returned about 60 years later. Folklore fills the time gap with amazing stories of the slab's wondrous virtues. It relates that thieves had tried to carry the slab away, but it miraculously gained weight until the thieves gave up and abandoned it on some waste ground. A mason recovered the stone and found it suitable for building. The Lucky Stone, however, did not like this prospect. It glowed, moved about, moaned and seemed to take on a human shape, until the workmen finally left it alone.[7]

The Wishing Stone, Fahan, County Donegal

The Wishing Stone is built into the wall beside the entrance to the old graveyard. To have a request granted, applicants would formulate the wish while they held a clenched fist into the hole. Fahan cemetery occupies the former site of a sixth-century monastery, but the Wishing Stone tradition is certainly of later origin. It started perhaps during the last few centuries, when the initial purpose of the stone in the wall was lost.[8]

**The Wishing Stone,
St Brigid's Cathedral,
County Kildare**

*The wishing ritual at St Brigid's
Cathedral is of rather recent
origin. It is said that if one
puts an arm through the
perforated stone that is built
into the wall as a cornerstone,
and touches his or her shoulder,
a wish will come true.*

Ireland's only wishing stone of international fame – the Blarney Stone – can look back on a long history before people began to kiss it as a talisman. Old traditions link the Blarney Stone firmly to kingship, and to the MacCarthy clan, once one of the most influential families in the south west of Ireland and the builders of Blarney Castle. Some claim that the stone was, in fact, part of the original Lia Fáil from Tara; others believe that the Blarney Stone was a segment of the Scottish inauguration stone of Scone, which came as a present from Robert Bruce to the MacCarthys in gratitude for Irish support in the 1314 Battle of Bannockburn. If there is a grain of truth in these stories, the Blarney Stone might well have begun its career as the inauguration stone of the MacCarthy clan.

The practise of kissing the stone in order to 'gain the gift of Irish eloquence' or, as a hostile observer remarked in 1789, 'the privilege of telling lies for seven years', was only introduced towards the end of the eighteenth century by James St John Jeffereys, whose family had acquired the estate around 1700. He obviously based the idea on the lore of Cormac Teige MacCarthy of Blarney, who sent persuasive but non-committal letters to Queen Elizabeth I in order to remain in control of his estates. The Queen's alleged remark that 'This is all Blarney, he never means what he says', instigated the initially derogatory term 'blarney' for meaningless talk. By Jeffereys' time, however, 'blarney' had become the description for the desired art of eloquence. Today, the Blarney Stone is one of Ireland's major tourist attractions. Hundreds of thousands of visitors annually climb the tower of Blarney Castle to kiss the magical stone for eloquence or as a talisman, and small portions of the 'original Blarney stone' can be acquired by visitors who wish to partake in the 'luck of the Irish'.[9]

The Blarney Stone, Blarney Castle, County Cork

Wishing Chairs and the Festival of Lughnasa

Stone chairs are the most popular wish-fulfilling stones in the northern half of the country. Once especially visited by women wishing to marry or conceive, they have long become trusted to fulfil any type of wish to both gender. A few of these wishing chairs belong to the Cailleach Bhéarra and to St Brigid,[10] but the majority of them are tightly linked to St Patrick and the festival of Lughnasa. St Patrick's wishing chairs occur for instance at Carrickatuke in County Armagh, near Downpatrick in County Down, and at Tobernalt and on Coney Island, both in County Sligo. According to the respective local traditions, the chairs can be visited at any time of the year, though they are said to be especially powerful at the time of Lughnasa.

The alignment of several megalithic monuments to the position of the sun around Lughnasa, and the association of the pre-Celtic land goddess Tailtiu with the festival, illustrate the antiquity of the harvest gatherings at the beginning of August. Myths relate that Tailtiu had died from exhaustion after clearing plains for cultivation, and that her foster son, the Celtic god Lugh, established the festival in her honour. With the Christian conquest, St Patrick took the patronage from Lugh, when at Lughnasa he reportedly destroyed the main pagan idol of Ireland, the Crom Dubh. Hence, the ancient harvest festival was transformed into a celebration of the Christian triumph, and would became widely known as *Domhnach Chrom Dubh* or the Sunday of Crom Dubh.[11]

Other popular designations mirror some of the festival customs and traditions, which continued into the early decades of the twentieth century: the term Fraughan or Bilberry Sunday recalls communal berry gatherings; the name Garland Sunday recalls the practice of decorating stones at the assembly sites; Height Sunday reflects the custom to climb the highest hill or mountain in the area; and *Lammas* derives from the old English 'Loaf Mass', a celebration of the corn crop and the harvest.

St Patrick's Chair, Altadaven, County Tyrone

Local tradition has it that the hillock in Altadaven Woods was a druidic ceremonial site before St Patrick preached from the stone chair and baptised converts in the well nearby.

The place has indeed been identified as an ancient site for Lughnasa assemblies; dubbed Blaeberry Sunday, the festival survived into the early twentieth century. The times of big communal celebrations in Altadaven Woods are gone, but individuals would still visit and climb the stone chair to make a wish, which supposedly will come true if it is not disclosed to anyone. Then, they might resort to the healing well nearby to cure various diseases, particularly warts. The votive offerings of rags, ribbons, medals and other objects left at the trees give evidence of the ongoing popularity of the place.[12]

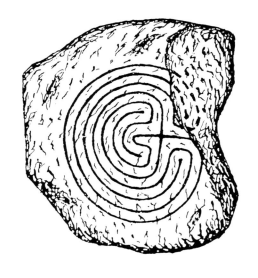

CONCLUSION

Christian and Pagan —
The Stone Cult in Modern Ireland

The industrialisation and modernisation of Irish society, together with the strict organisation of the Catholic Church, have undeniably led to a decline in popular religious observances and in the interest in ancient tales and legends. From the first decades of the twentieth century, when a systematic documentation of various folklore aspects had begun, informants often expressed their concerns that the old traditions were about to die and would hardly survive into the next generation.

Looking at the role of sacred stones in modern Ireland, we can luckily say that these predictions were too pessimistic. Certainly, there are sacred places and their stories which are almost entirely forgotten, even by those living nearby. And several formerly prominent pilgrimages, like the night-time stations at Glencolumbcille on 9 June, attract a steadily decreasing number of devotees.

Apparition Stones, Knock, County Mayo

The village of Knock in County Mayo appeared in modern Irish church history on a Thursday evening in 1879, when a group of people aged between six and 75 had a vision of the Virgin Mary on the south gable of the old local Church of St John the Baptist. Today, about 1,000,000 people come to visit the shrine each year, and a modern cathedral has long been erected to accommodate the constant flow of pilgrims. A portion of the Apparition Stones from the gable is built into the wall of an extension to the old church, and pilgrims touch the stones before blessing themselves as part of a visit to Knock Shrine.[1]

By and large, however, the veneration of sacred stones in the context of pilgrimage still flourishes, and the legends linking stones to saints are well remembered. Huge crowds undertake the mountain pilgrimage to Croagh Patrick, or visit St Brigid's Well and Shrine in Faughart, or come to pray in the cathedral of Knock. When pilgrims walk around the sacred stones at these sites, when they touch them, pass them around their bodies, or when they kneel down or lie on them to connect with the divine, they keep the ancient traditional rites and practices alive, even though they might often do so unconsciously.

From the most visited pilgrimage sites to the shrines of rather local significance, it is particularly the healing stones which still enjoy a considerable popularity, even beyond the official pattern days. People of different ages, gender and educational background visit individually to do their rounds, and to handle the sacred stones. Shiny coins and fresh flowers, rosaries, holy pictures and other offerings are left as tokens of their faith. In the south west of the country, the old practice to take scrapings from sacred stones has rather recently been revived and is spreading northwards. Using small pebbles as tools, pilgrims mark the sign of the cross in boulders, parts of church masonry or stone carvings. The scrapings are saved and taken in water, preferably from a holy well. This is a very intense way of connecting physically with a healing stone, and has its roots in the ancient belief in the curative qualities of dust from sacred stones.[2]

Pilgrim's Crosses, Gougane Barra, County Cork

Gougane Barra, closely associated with the sixth-century Saint Finbarr of Cork, is very popular with pilgrims and tourists alike. Several stone slabs at this beautiful shrine are scratched with crosses, although this practice is not mentioned in the note on the entrance describing the traditional performance of the 'rounds'.

Grave Slab, Ballyvourney, County Cork (right)

The monastic site of Ballyvourney, founded in the sixth or seventh century by St Gobnait, remains one of the most important pilgrimage sites in County Cork. The cross-inscribed stone slab in the churchyard marks the saint's grave.

Sheela-na-Gig, Kilsarkan, County Kerry (opposite page)

Kilsarkan Church in County Kerry is particularly visited during the month of May. Visitors of either gender scrape the sign of the cross into the carving of a Sheela-na-Gig and into other parts of the masonry.[3]

The last decade, too, saw the revival of open-air celebrations of Mass at sacred places around the country. Common venues are old monastic sites, holy wells, and – especially in the north and west – Mass Rocks or Penal Altars. A popular date for these congregations is the time around the ancient harvest festival of Lughnasa.

Lughnasa and the other principal feast days of pre-Christian Ireland are also considered particularly suitable to pay respect and reverence to prehistoric monuments and cult stones. An increasing number of people acknowledge the spiritual energy at those sacred places, and leave coins, fresh flowers, fruit or sea shells at stone circles, pillars, cairns and dolmens. They take up, or perhaps in some cases continue, the old practice of offerings to megalithic monuments which had been popular until the early decades of the nineteenth century. The reverence for sacred stones and stone monuments beyond the Christian context does not necessarily classify a person as an atheist or agnostic; it is, however, one characteristic trait of a modern spiritual concept or movement that is collectively known as Paganism or Neo-Paganism.[4]

In Europe, modern Paganism has its roots in the 1960s and 1970s. Several Pagan organisations revive archaic polytheistic religions, usually from their own historical backgrounds.[5] The most prominent movements in Ireland are Wicca (Witchcraft) and Neo-Druidism. While Wicca spirituality would focus on animistic beliefs and the ancient perceptions of the mother goddess, Neo-Druidism emphasises characteristically on Celtic rites and beliefs. As Pagan movements have no fixed buildings for their

**The Cailleach Bhéarra,
Kilcatherine, County Cork**
(right)

*In the lore of west Munster, the
Cailleach Bhéarra is firmly
linked with the Beara Peninsula
in County Cork, where several
prehistoric monuments or
natural features are assigned to
her. Particularly impressive is a
natural boulder on the coast
near Kilcatherine Point, which
some say is her stone chair,
while others claim is her petrified
self. The stone is a very popular
wishing stone or lucky talisman,
decorated all over with small
offerings of pebbles, flowers,
coins and medals.[6]*

**Idol Stones on Boa Island,
Lough Erne, County Fermanagh**
(opposite page)

*Caldragh Cemetery on Boa
Island is a powerful place,
guarded by two stone idols
from the transitional period
between paganism and early
Christianity. The two-faced
Janus figure seems to represent
a Celtic deity; the smaller
Lustymore Idol, called after the
site of its find, has sometimes
been likened to the carvings of
Sheela-na-Gigs. In recent years,
since the stones became revered
as lucky idols, visitors leave
coins as tokens.[7]*

worship, their followers would gather at places of pre-Christian religious or magic significance. Stone circles are especially valued, since the motif of the circle is generally held to represent the cycle of life.

Following a decline throughout the second half of the twentieth century, the interest in the popular lore of megalithic monuments is at present clearly increasing. It is a general phenomenon and not at all confined to modern Pagans. A comparison between recent renditions of myths and tales and those recorded until about 1950 show that modern versions would often significantly simplify a story, or even import motifs from different traditions. An example is the lore of the stone circle at Killarney in County Kerry. Around 1900, the monument was popularly explained as a giant family that had been petrified by a magician who

was tired of constantly fighting them. Today, they are taken as a family turned to stone for dancing on a Sunday. Valuable contributions to the preservation of the ancient lore of sacred stones and stone monuments are made by archaeological and historical societies and community groups with their projects on old traditions. The Office of Public Works in Dublin and the Department of the Environment and Heritage in Belfast aid the process when they incorporate folklore aspects in their descriptions of Ireland's national monuments.

With the ancient myths and legends kept alive, and Christian pilgrims and modern Pagans seeking the divine in the sacred landscape, revered stones and stone monuments are not just curious relics of the past or tourist attractions of merely historical and archaeological significance. They remain living parts of the cultural and spiritual heritage of Ireland. ▨

Notes and References

Introduction

1. See Ancient Laws of Ireland, Rolls Series, iv 142, v 472; gloss to the Bretha Comaithchesa (Judgements of Joint Tenancy); the same expression, i.e. *ailche adrada*, appears in the *Fastad Cirt ocus Dligid* (Confirmations of Right and Law); Macalister, R.A. Stewart, *The Archaeology of Ireland* (London, 1928/New York, 1977), p. 92; O'Kelly, Michael J., *Early Ireland. An Introduction to Irish Prehistory* (Cambridge, 1989/1997), p. 253.

2. Westropp, Thomas Johnson, *A Folklore Survey of County Clare* (Dublin, 1912), p. 69.

3. See Rees, Alwyn and Brinley, *Celtic Heritage. Ancient Tradition in Ireland and Wales* (London, 1961), pp. 26-80 for a very detailed study of the Cycles.

4. Ellis, Peter Beresford, *Celtic Women. Women in Celtic Society and Literature* (London, 1995), p. 21; Ó hÓgáin, Dáithí, *Myth, Legend & Romance. An Encyclopaedia of the Irish Folk Tradition* (London, 1990), pp. 312-3. Note: The earliest sections of the *Leabhar Gabhála* survived in a twelfth-century manuscript that was in turn based on a lost text from the eighth century. Fifty women and three men landed on the Dingle Peninsula in County Kerry; two of the men died shortly after their arrival and the women were drowned in the Flood; only Fintan survived in several guises into Christian times to relate the early history of Ireland. The tradition of Cessair is not contained in the *Leabhar Gabhála*.

5. Macalister, R.A. Stewart, ed., *Leabhar Gabhála Érenn* 1-5 (London, 1941), pp. 61–2, 73; O'Rahilly, Thomas F., *Early Irish History and Mythology* (Dublin, 1946), pp. 154–172; Rees, op. cit., pp. 118–139; Ó hÓgáin (1990), op. cit., pp. 312-3.

6. Note: On the Continent significant reforms from the eighth century onwards had succeeded in bringing about a well-organised Church under the sole authority of the Pope. The spiritual and structural independence of the Celtic Church, with her ancient traditions and rituals, was no longer compatible to the ideals of the Papacy. By the end of the eleventh century, there were calls for re-organisation and reform and, in 1111, the Synod of Cashel became the starting point for a rigorous reformatory initiative in Ireland. The earlier system of independent monasteries was dissolved and, instead, a diocesan system of parishes and bishoprics with centres in Armagh, Cashel, Dublin and Tuam was established. In 1142, the Cistercians were the first order to arrive from the Continent, soon followed by the Benedictines, Augustinians, Dominicans and Franciscans.

7. Connolly, S.J., *Priests and People in Pre-Famine Ireland, 1780-1845* (Dublin, 1982), pp. 113, 121-2.

8. Connolly (1982), op. cit., pp. 141, 148; Lee, Joseph, *The Modernisation of Irish Society 1848-1918* (Dublin, 1973), p. 43.

Goddess, Hags and Fairy Queens

1. Wood-Martin, W.G., *Traces of the Elder Faiths in Ireland: A Folklore Sketch. A Handbook of Irish Pre-Christian Traditions*, Vol. II (London/New York/Bombay, 1902), pp. 253-4.

2. Burl, Aubrey, *Rites of the Gods* (London/Melbourne/Toronto, 1981), p. 39; Eogan, George and Herity, Michael, *Ireland in Prehistory* (London/New York 1977/1989), pp. 15-24.

3. Note: Smaller graves co-existed with monumental tombs; it has been reckoned that the latter were exclusively built to bury the most important members of a tribe, or otherwise that some population groups preferred the simple sepulchral practice to the monumental. Harbison, Peter, *Guide to National Monuments in Ireland* (Dublin, 1979), p. 5; Macalister, R.A. Stewart, *The Archaeology of Ireland* (London, 1928/New York, 1977), p. 63; O'Kelly, Michael J., *Early Ireland. An Introduction to Irish Prehistory* (Cambridge, 1989/1997), pp. 85, 123, 127.

4. Ellis, Peter Beresford, *Celtic Women. Women in Celtic Society and Literature* (London, 1995), pp. 30-1.

5. Burl (1981), op. cit., p. 197; Dames, Michael, *Mythic Ireland* (London, 1992/1996), p. 55; Lett, Henry William, 'The Dun at Dorsey, Co. Armagh', in *JRSAI* 28, 1-14 (Dublin, 1898); Paterson, T.G.F., *Country Cracks. Old Tales from the County of Armagh* (Dundalk, 1939), p. 30.

    The custom to whitewash pillar stones has also been recorded from Edenmore, County Down and Carnalridge, County Derry. For Carnhill, Mullyash see MacNeill, Maire, *The Festival of Lughnasa* (Dublin 1962/1982), pp. 161-2; IFC 888:540-1; IFC 891:398-400, 463-70, 473-5.

6. Note: Fethard had initially four carved images of Sheela-na-Gigs. One of them was stolen in 1990 (local information).

7. Ó Crualaoich, Gearóid, Continuity and adaptation in legends of Cailleach Bhéarra, in *Béaloideas 56* (Dublin, 1988), pp. 153-4. Note: Medieval literature portrayed the Cailleach usually as an old woman of indefinite age. An emanation of a goddess of sovereignty, she would have taken numerous husbands. Among her royal spouses was Niall of the Nine Hostages, who unlike his brothers kissed and embraced the old and ugly Cailleach. She changed into a beautiful woman, and awarded Niall with the kingdom of Ireland.

8. Giraldus Cambrensis, ch. 88 in Gerald of Wales (Giraldus Cambrensis), *The History and Topography of Ireland*, ed. O'Meary, John J. (London, 1951/1982).

9. Keating, op. cit., I, p. 11. Note: Doubts remain about the identity of the fifth province. In early literature it has frequently been represented as a sub-division of Munster. Alternatively, the fifth province was held to be Meath (*Midhe*), created in the second century AD by King Tuathal Teachtmhar from a portion of each of the other provinces.

10. Only fragments survived of the decorated pillars from Derrykeighan, County Antrim, and Mullaghmast, County Kildare. According to popular tradition, the Killycluggin Stone, from County Cavan, has been venerated as a main pagan idol before it was destroyed by St Patrick. It is reconstructed now and belongs, like the Castlestrange Stone from County Roscommon, clearly to the omphalos type, while the Turoe stone seems to stand between the omphallic and phallic tradition. On Castlestrange see: Evans, Estyn, *Prehistoric and Early Christian Ireland. A Guide* (London, 1966), p. 183; Harbison (1979), op. cit., pp. 208-9; O'Kelly, op. cit., pp. 286-7; on Turoe see Bohan-Long, Rosaleen, *Stone Carvings of the Irish Iron Age* (Galway, n.y.), pp. 2-3; Macalister (1928/1977), op. cit., pp. 230-1; O'Kelly, op. cit., pp. 284-6, 288.

11. Macalister, R.A. Stewart, ed., *Leabhar Gabhála Éireann* 1-5 (London, 1941), pp. 61-2, 73. It is also known as the Cat Stone, for an alleged resemblance to a cat watching a mouse. This likeness, however, is hard to detect, even with imagination and the name seems to derive from another lost tradition.

12. Rees, op. cit., p. 159.

13. Note: On the Continent, the La Tène culture flourished throughout the last five centuries BC.

14. Ó hÓgáin (1990), op. cit., p. 312; Smyth, op. cit., p. 11.

15. Grinsell, Leslie V., *Folklore of Prehistoric Sites in Britain* (London, 1976), p. 43; Ó hÓgáin (1990), op. cit., pp. 67-69; Smyth, op. cit., p. 31.

16. Ó hÓgáin (1990), op. cit., pp. 185-190; Smyth, op. cit., p. 11.

17. Conwell, Eugene Alfred, *Discovery of the Tomb of Ollamh Fodhla* (Dublin, 1873); Dames, op. cit., p. 220; Macalister (1928/1977), op. cit., p. 307; McMann, Jean, *Loughcrew. The Cairns* (Oldcastle, 1993/2002), p. 20; Ó Crualaoich, op. cit., pp. 153-178; OSL Meath (1836), pp. 97-99; Wood-Martin, W.G., *Traces of the Elder Faiths in Ireland: A Folklore Sketch. A Handbook of Irish Pre-Christian Traditions*, Vol. II (London/New York/Bombay, 1902), p. 253; S 717:65; local information.

18. Note: Examples near Kilross, County Sligo, and near Dungarvan, County Waterford. On the Cailleach Bhéarra on Slieve Gullion see Burl (1981), op. cit., p. 81; Dames, op. cit., p. 55.

19. Note: The name Meadhbh translates as 'one who intoxicates'.
    Ellis, op. cit., pp. 41-45; Ó hÓgáin (1990), op. cit., pp. 293-5; Cowell, John, *Sligo – Land of Yeats' Desire. History, Literature, Folklore, Landscape* (Dublin, 1990), p. 19; Harbison (1979), op. cit., p. 217; O'Kelly, op. cit., p. 55; on the apparition Wood-Martin (1902), Vol I, op. cit., p. 369.

20. Eogan and Herity, op. cit, pp. 57-8 date the arrival of the passage grave builders to *c.* 2,500 BC. Ó hÓgáin, Dáithí, *The Sacred Isle. Belief and Religion in Pre-Christian Ireland* (Cork, 1999), p. 8; O'Kelly, op. cit., pp. 97-109.

21. Burl (1981), op. cit., p. 45; Eogan and Herity, op. cit., pp. 57, 67; Ó hÓgáin (1999), op. cit., pp. 9, 11.

22. Spring and autumn equinoxes fall on 20/21 March and 22/23 September; the term solstice derives from the Greek word for 'standing sun'; summer solstice is 21 July, winter solstice 21 December. On a study regarding the stone alignments in the south west see particularly Prendergast, F., 'Ancient Astronomical Alignments: Fact or Fiction?', in *Archaeology Ireland*, Vol 16/no 2, 32-35 (Dublin, 2002).

23. Note: In contemporary Europe, quartz has been rediscovered as a powerful healing stone for female complaints. On the use in Ireland see Burl (1981), op. cit., p. 93; McCann, op. cit., p. 27.

24. Burl, (1981), op. cit., pp. 82-3; Macalister (1928/1977), op. cit., pp. 99-103; Reden, Sybille von, *Die Megalith-Kulturen. Zeugnisse einer verschollenen Urreligion* (Köln, 1960/78), p. 86. Note: Irish passage grave art has been recorded from the Boyne Valley, Loughcrew, Fourknocks and Tara, all in County Meath; from the County Wicklow sites at Seefin, Baltinglass, and Tournant; from Sess Kilgreen and Knockmany, County Tyrone and from Carnanmore and Lyles Hill, County Antrim. The motifs were picked on the stone with flint or quartz points. Abroad, comparable ornamentations occur in considerable numbers in Brittany; they are scarce in England, Scotland and Wales and practically non-existent on the Continent. For detailed information on Bronze Age Rock Art see O'Kelly, op. cit., pp. 111-4.

25. AFM for the year 111 AD; Burl (1981), op. cit., p. 82; Coffey, Georg, Knockmany, in *JRSAI* 28, 93-111 (Dublin, 1898), pp. 93-111.

26. Today, Tailtin is usually associated with Teltown, which lies *c.* 15 miles from Loughcrew.

27. Harbison (1979), op. cit., p. 7, Macalister (1928/1977), op. cit., p. 75; O'Kelly, op. cit., pp. 92-4. Note: Considerable concentrations occur in the northern half, in the east between Counties Dublin and Waterford, and in the west in Counties Clare and Galway.

28. Hall, Mr and Mrs Samuel Carter, *Ireland. Its Scenery, Character etc.*, (1841), Vol. 1, p. 397.

29. Burl (1981), op. cit., p. 66; Ó hÓgáin (1990), op. cit., p. 213. Note: Donn means literarily dark or brown; Ó hÓgáin suggests that the romance might have been constructed around the archaic plot of the fight between darkness and light, or on the goddess lying with the heroic warrior.

30. Dames, op. cit., pp. 81-83.

31. Dames, op. cit., pp. 81-83; Dutton, Hely, *A Statistical Survey of the County of Clare* (Dublin, 1808), pp. 318-9; Rees, op. cit., p. 289; Wood-Martin (1902), Vol I; op. cit., pp. 348-9; Grinsell, op.cit., pp. 40-43; Ó hÓgáin (1990), op. cit., pp. 161-3. Note: also in short versions as Labby Rock for the dolmen in Carrickglass,

near Lough Arrow, Counry Sligo. In Scottish and English lore, their 'beds' would often be caves.

32. Information sign on site. Note: The structure is aligned with the setting sun at the spring and autumn equinoxes.

33. Dames, op. cit., pp. 52-3; OSL Donegal (1835), pp. 247-8. Note: In contrast to popular lore, O'Hanlon, John in *Lives of Irish Saints*, Vol I (Dublin, 1875) refers to Daveog or Beoc as a male saint and abbot of Lough Derg, who had possibly come to Ireland from Wales. According to Wood-Martin (1902), op. cit., Vol. II, p. 253, local people would alternatively attribute the stone to St Brigid and St Dabehoe [*sic*]; today, a partly collapsed Bronze Age structure on a nearby hillock is instead pointed out as St Daveaog's Chair. Local information (June 2000).

34. MacNeill, op. cit., pp. 160-1; Paterson, op. cit., p. 30; local information.

35. Conwell, op. cit.; Wood-Martin (1902), Vol II, op. cit., p. 253; S 717:65. Dames, op. cit., p. 220; Macalister (1928/1977), op. cit., p. 307; McMann, op. cit., p. 20; Ó Crualaoich, op. cit., pp. 153-178; OSL Meath (1836), pp. 97-99.

36. On the perceptions of the Cailleach see Ó hÓgáin (1990), op. cit., p. 67; Ellis, op. cit., p. 36.

37. Logan, Patrick, *The Holy Wells of Ireland* (London, 1980), p. 72; Ó hÓgáin (1990), op. cit., pp. 20-21; local information.

38. Ó hÓgáin (1990), op. cit., pp. 20-1; Smyth, op. cit., p. 18.

39. S 516:1f-I (1903), 213-6.

40. OSL Carlow (1839), p. 164; O'Toole, Edward, 'The Holy Wells of Co. Carlow', in *Béaloideas* 4/1, 3-23; 107-130 (Dublin, 1933), p. 5; on Modeligo see S 956:321. Patricia Lysaght argues that the banshee derives from the idea of the beautiful goddess of sovereignty who was traditionally associated with influential families, while the *badhbh* is more closely related to the dark aspect of a land goddess, and to the war goddess of ancient myths. The *badhbh* appears in a rather frightful manifestation and often maintains an association with water. Lysaght, Patricia, *The Banshee. The Irish Supernatural Death Messenger* (Dublin, 1986), pp. 191-218; Ó hÓgáin (1990), op. cit., pp. 45-6.

41. On Áine see Ó hÓgáin (1990), op. cit., p. 21; Smyth, op. cit., p. 18; on the Little Hag see Wood-Martin (1902), Vol I, op. cit., p. 372; on Clíodhna see Ó hÓgáin (1990), op. cit., pp. 90-92; IFC 42:130-3; IFC 98:268-86.

42. See Higgins, Jim, *Irish Mermaids* (Galway, 1995) for a detailed study of mermaid carvings, and Ó hÓgáin (1990), op. cit., pp. 186-7 on the mermaid in Irish folklore. Note: Both references are based on the tale of Liban as related in the *Leabhar-na-Huidré*. The story recalls that Liban survived in her chamber when the sudden eruption of Lough Neagh drowned her family. At her own wish, she changed into a

salmon, and swam the seas for 300 years. Following her capture, Liban was baptised and died shortly afterwards. See also AFM for the year 558; The Annals of Ulster date the capture of Liban to 571. Carvings of mermaids were common in Romanesque church architecture in Britain, but scarce and considerably later in Ireland.

43.   Note: In 1155, the Anglo-Norman king of England, Henry II, had received a papal licence to invade Ireland in order to secure the country for the Church and to aid the process of Church reforms. The pope in question was Adrian IV – the only English pope in history.

44.   Cowell, op. cit., pp. 178-9; S 164:10-11; S 165:18-21.

45.   In 1317 Richard de Ledrede, a Franciscan friar appointed bishop of Ossory, set up an inquisition to detect evidence of witchcraft in Ireland. With papal approval, he was determined to uproot any relics of native Brehon Laws, which were in conflict with doctrines of Rome, and to frighten particularly the Anglo-Irish and Irish upper class into submission to Rome. In 1324, Dame Alice Kyteler of Kilkenny found herself accused of heresy and witchcraft. When she fled from Ireland, the bishop arrested her household, and tortured and burnt her Irish maid, Petronilla. The maid, originally from County Meath, seems to be the only native Irish woman to be burnt at the stake as a witch. After a period of quiet, the Colonial Parliament passed a law against witchcraft in 1586. Victims of the ensuing trials were particularly women of Anglo-Irish or Protestant backgrounds. In the nineteenth century, however, women with medical knowledge and healing power became increasingly derogatively known as witches. The changed attitude towards wise and independent women reached its peak in 1895 with the murder of Bridget Cleary, who was burnt in her County Tipperary home for being a witch or a fairy-changeling. On the witch-hunt in Ireland see Ellis, op. cit., pp. 221, 226; Connolly, S.J., *Priests and People in Pre-Famine Ireland, 1780 1845* (Dublin, 1982), p. 115; on Bridget Cleary see Bourke, Angela, *The Burning of Bridget Cleary* (London, 1999).

46.   Madden, Gerard, *Holy Island. Jewel of the Lough* (n.y.), p. 24.

47.   Wood-Martin (1902), Vol. II, op. cit., p. 212.

48.   IFC 117:12-15 (1935, I/E) Note: I visited Meelick in June 2005, but failed to find the bullaun.

49.   Wood-Martin (1902), Vol II, op. cit., p. 247; information on site.

Heroes, Kings and Giants

1.   Knott, Mary John, *Two Months at Kilkee* (Dublin, 1836), p. 159.

2.   Note: This period of considerable change was marked by the presence of the Beaker people, who owe

their name to the characteristic bell-shaped pottery, which they used to bury with their dead in single graves. The origin of the people lies in the dark, with Beaker pottery being unearthed in most parts of Europe. The introduction of metalworking and stone circles to Ireland was long attributed to the Beaker people, who would have been attracted by the ore deposits of the country. Rather recent excavations brought these theories into dispute. On archaeological aspects see O'Kelly, Michael J., *Early Ireland. An Introduction to Irish Prehistory* (Cambridge, 1989/1997), p. 69 and O'Nualláin, Seán, *Stone Circles in Ireland* (Dublin, 1995), pp. 5-6.

3. On the finds in graves see Eogan, George and Herity, Michael, *Ireland in Prehistory* (London/New York 1977/1989), p. 193, on Bronze Age burial see O'Kelly, op. cit., pp. 189-214.

4. Dames, Michael, *Mythic Ireland* (London, 1992/1996), pp. 98-100.

5. Keating, Geoffrey, *The General History of Ireland*, ed. O'Connor, Dermod (Dublin, 1809), I, p. 11; Macalister, R.A. Stewart, ed., *Leabhar Gabhála Éireann* 1-5 (London, 1941), pp. 61-2, 73; O'Rahilly, Thomas F., *Early Irish History and Mythology* (Dublin, 1946), pp. 154-172; On the gifts of the Tuatha, see Ó hÓgáin, Dáithí, *Myth, Legend & Romance. An Encyclopaedia of the Irish Folk Tradition* (London, 1990), pp. 312-3.

6. Note: The same idea occurs with gateposts to homesteads and farms in rural Ireland. Remarkable examples of 'male' and 'female' gateposts exist in the Maghera and Downpatrick areas of County Down.

7. On archaeological aspects see O'Kelly, op. cit., pp. 232-239; Ò Nualláin, op. cit., p. 5.

8. To the dating of the Newgrange circle see O'Kelly, op. cit., pp. 141-2; Ó Nualláin, op. cit., p.6.

9. Ó Nualláin, op. cit, p. 13.

10. Burl, Aubrey, *A Guide to Stone Circles of Britain, Ireland and Brittany* (New Haven/London, 1995), pp. 218-9; Fahy, E.M., 'A recumbent-stone Circle at Drombeg, Co. Cork', in *JCHAS* 64, 1-27 (Cork, 1959); Franklin, D., 'Stone Circle near Glandore, Co. Cork', in *JCHAS* 9, 23-24 (Cork, 1903); Somerville, Boyle T., 'Notes on a Stone Circle in County Cork', in *JCHAS* 15, 104-108 (Cork, 1909). Drombeg is probably the best-known circle of the south Munster group. It is an example of a 'recumbent' circle, which is a circle with one axial stone arranged with the longer side lying horizontally instead of standing vertically. Ó Nualláin, op. cit., p. 36.

11. Grinsell, Leslie V., *Folklore of Prehistoric Sites in Britain* (London, 1976), pp. 54-6; Plummer, Charles, *Bethada Náem nÉrenn/Lives of Irish Saints* (Oxford, 1968), p. clxviif; Gerald of Wales (Giraldus Cambrensis), *The History and Topography of Ireland*, ed. O'Meary, John J. (London, 1951/1982), chap. 51.

12. Burl, Aubrey, *A Guide to Stone Circles of Britain, Ireland and Brittany* (New Haven/London, 1995), p. 241; on the Battle of Moytirra see also Ó hÓgáin (1990), op. cit., pp. 312-315; on Mesolithic rock paintings see Bradbery, Jean/Service, Alastair, *Megaliths and their Mysteries. The Standing Stones of Old Europe* (London,

1979), p. 43; local information May 2003. Note: The narrative is based on the eleventh-century text of the Battle of Magh Tuireadh or Moytirra. In the nineteenth century, antiquarians erroneously identified Magh Tuireadh with the stone circles of Cong, and the ancient myth became part of the local lore. Currently, scholars prefer to place the first battle in the Lough Arrow region of County Sligo, an area which popular lore links to the second Battle of Moytirra between the Tuatha Dé Danann and the Formorians.

13. For archaeological details on stone alignments see for instance O'Kelly, op. cit. pp. 230-234. Note: Concentrations of stone alignments survived in Counties Derry, Cavan, Fermanagh and Tyrone, and in Counties Cork and Kerry. Compared to the stone alignments in Brittany, Irish examples are small and reach a length of maximum 44 feet. Excavations at the monuments allow dating them to *c.* 1900 to *c.* 900 BC.

14. Evans, Estyn, *Prehistoric and Early Christian Ireland. A Guide* (London, 1966), p. 67; MacNeill, Máire, *The Festival of Lughnasa* (Dublin 1962/1982), p. 174; S 973:2, 4, 79.

15. Lankford, Éamon, *Cape Clear Island: Its People and Landscape* (Dublin, 1999), p. 17.

16. Rock art is not related to the very naturalistic Ice Age representations of hunting scenes, which were discovered in caves in Spain and France and dated to *c.* 30,000 or 40,000 BC.

17. O'Kelly, op. cit., pp. 239-242.

18. Nineteenth-century interpretations of rock art in Ireland and England as ancient maps of Iron Age forts and Neolithic tombs could be dismissed. From the late 1960s, Italian scientists carried out elaborate surveys on rock art from Pinerolo, Turin; they took the cup-marks for springs and water-places, the crosses for pre-historic settlements and the circles for enclosures – and found that the arrangement of the motifs correspond convincingly with the respective features in the surrounding landscape. Paturi, Felix R., *Zeugen der Vorzeit- Auf den Spuren europäischer Vergangenheit* (Düsseldorf/Wien, 1976), pp. 135-8; 161.

19. Graves, James, 'On a Boulder with presumably Pagan Carvings at Clonfinlough, King's Co.', in *JRSAI* 8, (Dublin, 1865), p. 354; Harbison (1979), op. cit., p. 120; S 812:4-7; 23-4.

20. Notes: Comparative studies reveal a remarkable resemblance between rock art motifs in Ireland and on the Continent, but the available data is not sufficient to reconstruct the influence from abroad. It is, however, very likely that the meaning of the motifs varied between the different societies. Interpretations in the European context vary as well. Some commentators have suggested that the drilling of the holes was in itself regarded an act of magic; others considered that the pulverised stones were ascribed special healing virtues. The fact that well into the twentieth century, farmers in some coastal areas of Scotland left milk in cup-marked stones at certain times of the year was used to corroborate theories that the holes were initially meant to contain offerings to the spirits. Harbison (1979), op. cit., pp. 6-7; Macalister, R.A. Stewart, *The Archeology of Ireland* (London, 1928/New York, 1977), p.97; O'Kelly, op. cit., pp. 111-4; 239-242; Paturi,

op. cit., p. 154; Reden, Sybille von, *Die Megalith-Kulturen. Zeugnisse einer verschollenen Urreligion* (Köln, 1960/78), pp. 324-328.

21. Westropp, Thomas Johnson, 'The Cists, Dolmens and Pillars in the Eastern Half of the County of Clare', in *PRIA* 24, (Dublin, 1902), p. 84. Note: Standing stones might have been erected to mark routes or territories. Old Irish law tracts refer to the custom to define boundaries with pillar-stones, and to landmarks in the form of 'stones of adoration'.

22. For a comprehensive study of the heroic tradition see Ó hÓgáin, *The Hero in Irish Folk History* (Dublin, 1985), or Rees, op. cit. pp. 26-80.

23. Ó hÓgáin (1990), op. cit., pp. 312-315; local information (Neale information centre).

24. Ó hÓgáin (1990), op. cit., p. 414; Rees, op. cit., p. 67 dates the text on Cúchulainn's death to the ninth century.

25. The scene of Cúchullain's death is immortalised by Sheppard's sculpture in the GPO in Dublin, and on the village crest of Knockbridge. Harbison (1979), op. cit., p. 161; Ó hÓgáin (1990), op. cit., p. 136; Rees, op. cit., p. 332; S 665:366.

26. Herity, Michael, *Rathcroghan and Carnfree. Celtic Royal Sites in Roscommon* (Dublin, 1991), p. 13; Macalister (1928/1977), op. cit., p. 308.

27. Harbison (1979), op. cit., p. 209; Ó hÓgáin (1990),op. cit., pp. 147-8. Note: Excavations in 1913 and 1988 failed to find any traces of a burial. Herity (1991), op. cit., p. 19.

28. Evans, Estyn, *Prehistoric and Early Christian Ireland. A Guide* (London, 1966), p. 63; Harbison, Peter, *Guide to National Monuments in Ireland* (Dublin, 1979), p. 32; Keating, Geoffrey, *The General History of Ireland*, ed. O' Connor, Dermod (Dublin, 1809), I, p. 477; Logan, op. cit., p. 105; Ó hÓgáin (1990), op. cit., p. 323; Westropp, Thomas Johnson, 'Pillar-stone and Hole-stone, Co. Carlow', in *JRSAI* 17 (Dublin, 1997), p.90; IFC 407:58 (1910/11); S 910:112.

29. Notes: The AFM date the battle to the year 998, the Annals of Tighernach and the Annals of Inisfallen to 999. The site of the battle is disputed; today historians prefer to place it the plain between Kill, County Kildare and Saggart, County Dublin, or in the adjacent mountainous area. A reference to the Viking tradition to erect memorial stones to their dead appears in the poetical Edda, The Sayings of Hár, v. 72. 'To have a son is good, late though he be, and born when buried his father; stones see'st thou seldom set by the road-side but by kith raised over kinsmen *[sic]*.'

30. AFM for the year 998; Newman, Roger Chatterton, *Brian Boru. King of Ireland* (Dublin, 1983), pp. 112-114; Walshe, Patrick T., 'The Antiquities of the Dunlavin-Donard District', in *JRSAI* 61 (Dublin, 1931), pp. 134-5;S 914:222.

31. *The Irish Sword*, reply; Vol. 5, 266-7; Irwin, Liam, 'The Treaty of Limerick', in Jim Kemmy, ed., *The Limerick*

Anthology, 230-232; (Dublin, 1996), pp. 230-232; Hall, *Mr and Mrs Samuel Carter, Ireland. Its Scenery, Character* etc., (1841), Vol 1, p. 332. Note: French troops had supported the Irish during the Siege of Limerick. France too holds the tradition of a Limerick Treaty Stone. In 1907, they erected a Celtic Cross on a granite base in Fonteney, and the inscription on the base curiously informs that it was on this stone that the treaty was signed by which religious liberty had been promised to the Irish people.

32. Simms, J.G., *The Treaty of Limerick* (Dublin, 1961).

33. Note: The Fenian tales were particularly popular among Gaelic speakers in Ireland and Scotland; in the Scottish traditions, Finn figures as Fingal. See also Grinsell, op. cit., pp. 40-1.

34. Ó hÓgáin (1990), op. cit., pp. 213-223; Ó hÓgáin, Dáithí, *The Sacred Isle. Belief and Religion in Pre-Christian Ireland* (Cork, 1999), pp. 118-9; for a comprehensive study see Ó hÓgáin, *Fionn mac Cumhaill* (Dublin, 1988). Note: The literary Fionn died around 280 AD in a battle at the Boyne River.

35. Kennedy, Joseph, *The Monastic Heritage and Folklore of County Laois* (Roscrea, 2003), p. 158; Roe, Helen M., 'Tales, Customs and Beliefs from Laoighis', in *Béaloideas* 9, (Dublin, 1939), p. 24.

36. Cowell, John, *Sligo – Land of Yeats' Desire. History, Literature, Folklore, Landscape* (Dublin, 1990), p. 180; S 164:115.

37. Evans (1966), op. cit., p. 138; O'Kelly, op. cit., p. 229; Leask, H.G., 'The Long Stone, Punchestown, Co. Kildare', in *JRSAI* 67, (Dublin, 1937), pp. 250-252; Omurethi, 'Notes of Punchestown and Cradockstown', in *JKAS* 2, (Dublin, 1906-1908), pp. 37-46; S 776:289, 347. Notes: Further examples of Bronze Age long stones stand in Carrownacaw and Drumnahare, both in County Down, near Cullen in County Tipperary. The tallest European monolith is the prostrate Menhir of Locmanaquer, near Carnac in Brittany. It stood *c.* 66ft high.

38. Note: The concept of the supernatural heroic ability to leave imprints in stone should later be inherited by saints and missionaries of the early Celtic Church.

39. Wood-Martin, W.G., *Traces of the Elder Faiths in Ireland: A Folklore Sketch. A Handbook of Irish Pre-Christian Traditions*, (London/New York/Bombay, 1902), Vol. I, p. 163. Notes: The Bellanascaddan stone is, in fact, a cup-marked Bronze Age pillar. Scarce are giants' footprints in stone, as for instance in the Holy Stone in Donaghmore, Brittas, County Dublin. Footprints are primarily attributed to the mythical ancestors or clans and septs, and feature in the inauguration ceremonies of Gaelic chieftains and kings. Fionn's Stone, Barnameenagh, Leitrim, slopes of Slieve Anierin.

40. Meehan, op. cit., p. 369; local information.

41. Danaher, Kevin, *The Year in Ireland. A Calendar* (Cork, 1972), p. 121; Grinsell, op. cit, pp. 56-59; on the Cloghmore local information.

42. Wood-Martin (1902), Vol I, op. cit., pp. 351–2.

43. Fitzgerald, Walter, 'The Kernanstown (or Browne's Hill) Cromlech, County Carlow', in *JKAS* 5 (Dublin, 1906-1908), pp. 339-343; Glynn, Fiona, ed., *A Sense of Carlow. A collection of Local Folklore and Myth* (Carlow, 1997), p. 6; OSL Carlow (1839), p. 94. Note: The capstone is *c.* 24 feet long; and between 4 and-6 feet thick.

44. Lowry-Corry, Dorothy, 'Cairns at Corracloora, Co. Leitrim', in *JRSAI* 67, (Dublin, 1937), pp.302-303. Note: The grave belongs to the Neolithic period and is dated to *c.* 2,000 BC.

45. On Brú na Bóinne, Carnfree and Slievenamon see Meehan, op. cit., p. 217 and Ó hÓgáin (1990), op. cit., p. 39; Smyth, Daragh, *A Guide to Irish Mythology* (Dublin, 1988/1996), p. 11. On Fionn and Oísín see Dames, op. cit., p. 55; Smyth, op. cit., p. 70 . Note: The cairn is destroyed. Another tradition has Oísín buried under a pillar stone on Curran Mountain, Manorhamilton. County Leitrim.

46. Wood-Martin (1902), Vol I, op. cit., p. 352.

47. Meehan, op. cit., p. 177; local information Causeway information centre, visit March 2002.

48. Wood-Martin (1902), Vol I, op. cit., p.374.

49. Wood-Martin (1902), Vol II, op. cit., p. 219.

50. Note: Today, the stones are more popularly interpreted as parents and children, petrified for dancing on a Sunday. Wood-Martin (1902), Vol II, op. cit., pp. 219-221.

51. The Viking period in Ireland began in 795 with the Norse raid of Lambeg Island in Dublin Bay and the plundering of the monastic settlements of Inishmurray and Inisbofin off the west coast. Initially focussing on the coastline, Norse and Danish Vikings soon discovered the rivers Boyne, Erne, Liffey and Shannon to venture inland.

Saints, Sinners and Stone Slabs of Heaven

1. Chochrane, Robert, 'Notes on the Structures in the County of Cork rested in the Board of Works for Preservation as Ancient Monuments', in *JCHAS* 18, (Cork, 1912), pp. 3-4; Lankford, Éamon, *Naomh Ciarán. Pilgrim Islander* (Cork, 2000), pp. 26-28; Ó hÓgáin, Dáithí, *Myth, Legend & Romance. An Encyclopaedia of the Irish Folk Tradition* (London, 1990), p. 90; IFC 609:292 (I); S 295:152; 153-4 (I).

2. On links to Rome and Pre-Patrician missionaries see de Paor, Liam, *Saint Patrick's World* (Dublin, 1993), pp. 38-9; and Di Martino, Vittorio, *Roman Ireland* (Cork, 2003), pp. 154-5; Lankford, op. cit., p. 611 respectively.

3. Paterson, 146; Wood Wood-Martin, W.G., *Traces of the Elder Faiths in Ireland: A Folklore Sketch.* A

Handbook of Irish Pre-Christian Traditions (London/New York/Bombay, 1902), Vol I, p. 263.

4. On Irish monasteries of the early Celtic Church see de Paor, Liam and Máire, *Early Christian Ireland* (London, 1958/1978), pp. 50-1.

5. Note: The former is preserved in the National Museum in Dublin, the latter in Colmcille's Heritage Centre, Gartan, County Donegal. Ó hÓgáin, Dáithí, *The Sacred Isle. Belief and Religion in Pre-Christian Ireland* (Cork, 1999), pp. 50-54; O'Kelly, Michael J., *Early Ireland. An Introduction to Irish Prehistory* (Cambridge, 1989/1997), pp. 292, 294.

6. Rynne, Etienne, 'The Tau-Cross at Killinaboy. Pagan or Christian', in *North Munster Studies*, pp. 146-165 (Limerick, 1967); O'Kelly, op. cit., p. 289.

7. Harbison, Peter, *Guide to National Monuments in Ireland* (Dublin, 1979), p. 11; Ó hÓgáin (1999), op. cit., p. 350; O'Kelly, op. cit., pp. 250-2.

8. Chambers, Richard, *White Island. History and Mystery* (Fintona, 2002), pp. 32-37; Kelly, Eamonn P., *Sheela-na-Gigs. Origins and Function* (Dublin, 1996), p. 293; Macalister, R.A. Stewart, *The Archaeology of Ireland* (London, 1928/New York, 1977), p. 357.

9. Logan, Patrick, *The Holy Wells of Ireland* (London, 1980), p. 106.

10. Note: Some 300 Ogham inscribed pillars have survived in Ireland. Abroad, Ogham-inscribed stones occur exclusively in some areas of Irish settlements in Wales and Scotland. de Paor (1993), op. cit., p. 61; Macalister (1928/1977), op. cit., pp. 329-343, proposed the pagan interpretation of Ogham stones as embodiments of the essence or spirit of the person named on it; Harbison (1979), op. cit., p. 205, connects them to early Christian pilgrimage routes and suggests that the stones were inscribed to commemorate pilgrims.

11. Harbison (1979), op. cit., p. 13; Lydon, James, *The Making of Ireland. From Ancient Times to the Present* (London/New York, 1998), pp. 20-36; see Ó hÓgáin (1990), op. cit., pp. 324-5 for Vikings in folklore. Foote, Peter.G./Wilson, David.M., *The Viking Achievement* (London, 1970); Newman, op. cit.; ; on runic script see Teathbha, Vol. II, 1983. Runic inscriptions in Ireland are rare. Apart from the Killaloe stone, further examples were found on the Great Blasket and at Beginish, County Kerry, and at Nendrum, County Down, dated to the eleventh and twelfth century, see also de Paor (1958/78), op. cit., p. 162.

12. Ó hÓgáin (1990),op. cit., p. 195; Plummer, Charles, *Bethada Náem nÉrenn/Lives of Irish Saints* (Oxford, 1968), pp. clv-clxxviii.

13. Deuteronomy, 12.

14. MacNeill, Máire, The Festival of Lughnasa (Dublin 1962/1982), p. 602; Ó hÓgáin (1990), op. cit. pp. 194-6.

15. Meehan, Cary, *The Traveller's Guide to Sacred Ireland* (Glastonbury, 2004), p. 97.

16. Burl, Aubrey, *A Guide to Stone Circles of Britain, Ireland and Brittany* (New Haven/London, 1995), pp.

211-2; Evans, Estyn, *Prehistoric and Early Christian Ireland. A Guide* (London, 1966), p. 67; O'Kelly, op. cit., pp. 287-8; Macalister, R.A. Stewart, 'On a Stone with La Tène Decorations recently discovered in Co. Cavan', in *JRSAI* 52, (Dublin, 1922) p. 114 Ó Riordáin, Séan P., 'Fragment of the Killycluggin Stone', in *JRSAI* 82, 68-69 (Dublin, 1952); Raftery, Barry, 'Excavations at Killicluggin, Co. Cavan', in *UJA* 41, 49-54 (Belfast, 1978); For archaeological details see O'Kelly, op. cit., p. 288. Note: A biography of St Patrick from the ninth century, and an eleventh-century text provide corresponding descriptions of the Cenn Cruaich or Crom Cruach in Magh Sléacht. The Killycluggin Stone that stands on the roadside near Ballyconnell is a replica; the original is on display in the Cavan County Museum in Ballyjamesduff.

17. Dames, Michael, *Mythic Ireland* (London, 1992/1996), p. 77; Evans (1966), op. cit., p. 177; Lynch, J.F., Lough Gur, in *JCHAS* 1; (Cork 1895), pp.289-305; MacNeill, op. cit., p. 344.

18. Note: One pillar at Clonmacnoise, one of the Carndonagh stele and possibly one of the pillars on Boa Island, Fermanagh feature horned deities.

19. Wood-Martin (1902), Vol. I, op. cit., p.214.

20. Paterson; local information.

21. Harbison (1979), op. cit., p. 5; Ó hÓgáin (1999), op. cit., p. 7; O'Kelly, op. cit., pp. 5, 85-92. Note: Court tombs were originally covered by a stone mound or cairn. They usually contain multiple burials, both cremated and inhumed. Objects of practical use, for instance pottery, tools and projectile heads, were frequently interred with the human remains; personal gravegoods are scarce. The characteristic semi-circular area or court in front of the grave chamber suggests burial rituals; the recurrent orientation of the entrance towards the rising sun indicates solar worship.

22. Wood-Martin (1902) Vol I, op. cit., pp. 209, 211.

23. Westropp, Thomas Johnson, *A Folklore Survey of County Clare and County Clare Folk-Tales and Myths* (Dublin, 1910-1913), ed. Comber, Maureen, CLASP (Ennis, 2000), p. 94; 3.6.205, local information.

24. Dames, op. cit., p. 114; MacNeill, op. cit. pp. 268-275; IFC 466:283-4; IFC 888:359-60, 528-39, 542-3.

25. Ó hÓgáin (1990), op. cit., p. 69; OSL Cavan/Leitrim (1836), pp. 182-4.

26. Bigger, Francis Joseph, 'The Lake and Church of Kilmakilloge, the Ancient Church, Holy Well, and Bullán-stone of Temple Feaghna, and the Holy Well and Shrine of St. Finan´s, Co. Kerry', in *JRSAI* 28, 314-324 (Dublin, 1898), Crawford, Henry S., 'Notes on Stones used as a Cure at Killery, near Dromahair, and on certain Bullauns', in *JRSAI* 43 (Dublin, 1913), p. 268; Crozier, Isabel R/Rea, Lily C., 'Bullauns and other Basin Stones', in *UJA* 3 (Belfast, 1940), p.106; Evans (1966), op. cit., p. 130; Hall, Mr and Mrs Samuel Carter, *Ireland. Its Scenery, Character etc.*, Vol 1 (1841), pp. 121-2; Price, Liam, 'Rock-Basins, or "Bullauns" at Glendalough and elsewhere', in *JRSAI* 89 (Dublin, 1959), p. 167; Wakeman, (1874/75), op.

cit., pp. 459-460; IFC 466:10-11 (1934). Note: From their resemblance to St Brigid's Cursing Stone in Blacklion, County Cavan, nineteenth-century antiquarians gathered that they too were used in destructive semi-magic rituals. These theories have no foundation in local tradition.

27. Local information

28. Wakeman, W.F., 'On Certain Markings in Rocks, Pillar-stones, and Other Monuments Chiefly in the County of Fermanagh', in *JRSAI* 13 (Dublin 1874/5), pp. 459-460; IFC 466:10-11 (1934); Pagans and Wiccans (www.irishwitch.org, p. 6). Note: Meehan, op. cit., pp. 479-482 suggests that stones were placed in churn to increase milk profit.

29. MacNeill, op. cit., pp. 642-3; Nuttall Smith, G., 'Holy Well and Antiquities near Cahir, Co. Tipperary', in *JRSAI* 29 (Dublin, 1899), p. 258; OSL Tipp III, 1840, pp. 195-205; S 576:78f; 80; 87; local information, visit June 2005. Note: A different link of St Peakaun's to butter appears in folklore accounts from the 1930s which recall that long ago the water of the well turned to blood when a woman profaned it by washing butter in it.

30. Grinsell, Leslie V., *Folklore of Prehistoric Sites in Britain* (London, 1976), pp. 54-6; Plummer, Charles, *Bethada Náem nÉrenn/Lives of Irish Saints* (Oxford, 1968), pp. clxviif.

31. Crozier/Rea, op. cit.,p. 105.

32. Burl, Aubrey, A *Guide to Stone Circles of Britain, Ireland and Brittany* (New Haven/London, 1995), p.248, Harbison (1979), op. cit., p. 258; Walshe, Patrick T., 'The Antiquities of the Dunlavin-Donard District', in *JRSAI* 61 (Dublin, 1931), p. 128; S 914:8, 223. Note: the Piper's Stones in Irish folklore are usually linked to bag-pipe music. The earliest surviving musical instrument found in north-western Europe was a pipe carved from a swan's bone in England, see Bradbery, Jean/Service, Alastair, *Megaliths and their Mysteries. The Standing Stones of Old Europe* (London, 1979), p. 43.

33. Note: On the Continent imprint stones have frequently been taken over by the Cult of the Virgin Mary, and became linked to tales of the Holy Family passing the respective area on their flight to Egypt. In contrast to the religious lore in Europe, Irish saints did not use their power to actually perforate stones.

34. Kennedy, Joseph, *The Monastic Heritage and Folklore of County Laois* (Roscrea, 2003), p. 104; Ó hÓgáin (1990), op. cit., pp. 300-1; local information.

35. Local information from well keeper and notice on site, 17.8.2003.

36. O'Hanlon, John, *Lives of the Irish Saints* (Dublin, 1875), Vol. VI, p. 669.

37. Local information (September 2003).

38. de Paor (1993), op. cit., pp. 253-4; Evans (1966), op. cit., p. 206; Harbison, Peter, *Pilgrimage in Ireland. The Monuments and the People* (London, 1991), p. 136; Logan, op. cit., p. 8; Ó hÓgáin (1990), op. cit.,

pp. 152-3; IFC 84: 8-10 (1932); IFC 259:54-68 (1936); S 643:76 (I); local information.

39.   For Inishmore see IFC 305:452-3 (I; 1937); for Culdaff see Logan, op. cit., p. 105; for Carn see ibid, p. 103; IFC 96:320 (1952); S 897:2.

40.   Logan, op. cit., p. 104; Wakeman, W.F., 'Three Days on the Shannon. From Limerick to Lough Key' (Dublin, 1852) published in *Béaloideas* XI, (Dublin, 1941), p. 47; S 643:76 (I).

41.   Corlett, Christiaan, *Antiquities of West Mayo* (Wicklow, 2001).

42.   On the Catholic Church during the Cromwellian Era see Lydon, James, *The Making of Ireland. From Ancient Times to the Present* (London/New York, 1998), pp. 193-4.

43.   IFC 467:190; IFC 889: 47, 49-50,160,171,175,193; IFC 891:417; S 176:182, 192; S 177:59; S 178:187.

44.   Local information.

Stones of Kingship

1.   Spenser, Edmund, *A View of the Present State of Ireland*, ed. Renwick, W.L. (Oxford, 1970), p. 7.

2.   Note: The tree of Magh Adhair, which belonged together with a monolith and a bullaun stone to the inauguration site of the kings of Thomond in County Clare, was famous. Several kings of the *Dál Cais* (Dalcassian) and Ó Brien septs were installed at Magh Adhair, among them Brian Boru. For detailed information on inaugurations see, for instance, Macalister, R.A. Stewart, *The Archaeology of Ireland* (London, 1928/New York, 1977), pp. 306-310, and Fitzpatrick, Elizabeth, *Royal Inauguration in Gaelic Ireland c. 1100–1600. A Cultural Landscape Study* (Woodbridge, 2004).

3.   Evans, Estyn, *Prehistoric and Early Christian Ireland. A Guide* (London, 1966), p- 153; OSL Derry (1837), 233-4. Notes: The leading local clan would have taken the stone with them when they deserted Aileach in the twelfth century; later, when its history was lost, people would have linked it to St Colmcille as the most popular saint of the district.

4.   Hore, Herbert F., 'Inaugurations of Irish Chiefs', in *UJA* 1/5, (Belfast, 1857), p. 222.

5.   Macalister (1928/1977), op. cit., pp .308-9.

6.   Gwynn, Lucius, '*De Shil Chonaire Móir*', in *Ériu* 6, (Dublin 1922), pp. 139, 142; Ó hÓgáin, Dáithí, *Myth, Legend and Romance. An Encyclopaedia of the Irish Folk Tradition* (London, 1990), p. 158; Rees, Alwyn and Brinley, *Celtic Heritage. Ancient Tradition in Ireland and Wales* (London, 1961), p. 146.

7.   Rees, op. cit., p. 146; Stokes, Whitley, 'The Prose Tales of the *Dindshenchas*', in *RC* 15, (Dublin, 1894), p. 286.

8. Concannon, Maureen, *The Sacred Whore. Sheela, Goddess of the Celts* (Cork, 2004), pp. 60, 82-3.

9. Ó hÓgáin (1990), op. cit., p. 195; Rees, op. cit., p. 147.

10. Evans (1966), op. cit., p. 176; Macalister (1928/1977), op. cit., pp. 308-9; Ó hÓgáin (1990), op. cit., p. 326; Rees, op. cit., p. 165; Wood-Martin, W.G., *Traces of the Elder Faiths in Ireland: A Folklore Sketch. A Handbook of Irish Pre-Christian Traditions*, (London/New York/Bombay, 1902), Vol II, p. 258; local information 18.8.2003. Notes: Historians doubt the stone's ability to articulate itself, and suggest attributing the cry to a 'bull-roarer', that is, a piece of wood attached to a string, which would have been swung around out of sight of the congregation at the crowing ceremony. Bod Forghasa has been transferred from a nearby mound to its present location where it commemorates those slain at Tara during the rebellion of 1798.

11. Keating, Geoffrey, *The General History of Ireland*, ed. O'Connor, Dermod (Dublin, 1809), I, 3-4; Wood-Martin (1902), op. cit., Vol II, p. 257.

12. Crawley, Ernest, *The Oath, The Curse and The Blessing* (London, 1934), p. 46; Frazer, James George, *The Golden Bough. A Study in Magic and Religion* (London, 1974), p. 43; Hutton, Ronald, *The Pagan Religions of the Ancient British Isles. Their Nature and Legacy* (Oxford/Cambridge,USA, 1991/1997), p. 173. Note: Modern Carinthia corresponds with the Celtic kingdom of Noricum. The custom to install local dukes on the inauguration stone survived until the medieval period.

13. For Leac Mhic Eochadha, and Leck, County Monaghan see Hamilton, Gustavus E., 'Two Ulster Inauguration Places', in *JRSAI* 42, 64-66 (Dublin, 1912); On Cadamstown see Heany, Paddy, *At the Foot of Sieve Bloom. History and Folklore of Cadamstown* (n.y.), p. 10; on Warrenpoint see information brochure Newry and Mourne District Council, pp. 9, 32.

14. Hore, op. cit., pp. 221-3; Ó hÓgáin, Dáithí, *The Sacred Isle. Belief and Religion in Pre-Christian Ireland* (Cork, 1999), p. 166; AFM for the year 1448; Referring to the inauguration of Felim O'Conor in the year 1310, the Annals of Connacht note that '… this was the most splendid kingship-marriage ever celebrated in Connacht down to that day'. Herity, Michael, *Rathcroghan and Carnfree. Celtic Royal Sites in Roscommon* (Dublin, 1991), pp. 26, 28-29; Macalister (1928/1977), op. cit., p. 307; on Fraech see Ó hÓgáin (1990), op. cit., p. 233-5 and Smyth, Daragh, *A Guide to Irish Mythology* (Dublin, 1988/1996), pp. 74-5.

15. Notes: Fragments of the inauguration stone were allegedly kept in an orchard near Tullahoge but had been carried away by the end of the eighteenth century. AFM for the year 1432.

16. Frazer, W., 'The Clandeboy O'Neill's Stone Inauguration Chair, now preserved in the Belfast Museum', in *JRSAI* 28, (Dublin, 1898), pp. 254-256; Harbison, Peter, *Guide to National Monuments in Ireland* (Dublin, 1979), p. 11; Macalister (1928/1977), op. cit., p. 307; Ó hÓgáin (1990), op. cit., p. 37; Wood-Martin (1902),op. cit., Vol II, pp. 251-252.

Stones of Truth and Justice

1. Hall, Mr and Mrs Samuel Carter, *Ireland. Its Scenery, Character etc.*, (1841-1843), Vol 1, p. 308.

2. Wood-Martin (1902), op. cit., Vol. II, p. 224 Notes: The commentary stems from McGuire, canon of Armagh. The hillfort of Rathmore, near the cathedral, was reportedly the inauguration place of the kings of Oriel. Information in Clogher Cathedral.

3. Hall, op. cit., Vol 1; p. 308; OSL Waterford (1841), 59f.

4. On Farranglogh see Conwell, Eugene Alfred, *Discovery of the Tomb of Ollamh Fodhla* (Dublin, 1873), pp. 1-3; McMann, Jean, *Loughcrew. The Cairns* (Oldcastle,1993/2002), p. 9; Wood-Martin, W.G., *Traces of the Elder Faiths in Ireland: A Folklore Sketch. A Handbook of Irish Pre-Christian Traditions,* (London/ New York/Bombay, 1902), Vol II, pp. 222-3.

5. Logan, Patrick, *The Holy Wells of Ireland* (London, 1980), p. 109, quoting Bishop Dive Downes.

6. Hyde, Douglas, *The Stone of Truth and other Irish Folktales* (Dublin, 1979), pp. 21-25; OSL Mayo (183) II, 38; Otway, Caesar, *A Tour in Connaught* (Dublin, 1839), pp. 236-241; Wilde, William R., 'Memoir of Gabriel Beranger, and his Labours in the Cause of Irish Art, Literature, and Antiquities from 1760-1780', in *JRSAI* 2, (Dublin, 1870/71), pp. 135-6; Wilde, William R., *Lough Corrib, its Shores and Islands* (Dublin/ London, 1872), p. 267; Wood-Martin (1902), op. cit., Vol II, pp. 65-66.

7. IFC 669: 369-72 (1939; I); local information.

8. Ní Mhóráin, Muireann, *Clocha Mallachta na hÉireann* (unpubl. Ms, DIF, Dublin, 1979), p. 76; OSL Mayo (1838), I, 234-5; Rolleston, T.W., 'The Church of St. Patrick on Caher Island, County Mayo', in *JRSAI* 29, (Dublin, 1900), p. 357; Wood-Martin (1902), op. cit., Vol II, p. 106.

9. Evans, Estyn, *Prehistoric and Early Christian Ireland. A Guide* (London, 1966), p. 64; Fitzgerald, Walter, 'The Round Tower and Holed Stone of Castledermot', in *JRSAI* 22, (Dublin, 1892), pp. 66-69; Logan, op. cit., pp.10-11; S 782:82; information sign on site. Note: The monastery of Castledermot was founded in 812 by St Diarmaid. The swearing stone has almost sunk into the ground, before it was re-erected as a head-stone in 1889. In the same graveyard lies the only hog-backed Viking grave-marker that has yet been discovered in Ireland.

10. Corlett, Christiaan, *Antiquities of West Mayo* (Wicklow, 2001), p. 47 quoting Otway; Kelly (1897), 185-6; Ní Mhóráin, op. cit., p. 71; OSL Mayo (1838), I, 236; on Druid's Stone see S 95:147-8. Note: A few years ago, the flag was signposted as a National Monument. Today, the sign has been removed, the area is fenced off, and the stone is no longer accessible to the public; visits 1999, 2002, 2004.

11. Evans, Estyn, *Irish Folk Ways* (London 1957/1989), p. 300. Ó hÓgáin, Dáithí, *The Sacred Isle. Belief and Religion in Pre-Christian Ireland* (Cork, 1999), pp. 212-3.

12. Ferguson, Samuel, 'The Burial of King Cormac', in *Lays of the Western Gael and other poems*, (London, 1865), pp. 54-59.

13. Betha Máedóc Ferna (II)/'Life of Maedoc of Ferns' (II) ff 168a-218b, in Plummer, Charles, *Bethada Náem nÉrenn/Lives of Irish Saints* (Oxford, 1968).

14. Ó hÓgáin (1999), op. cit., p. 211; Rees, Alwyn and Brinley, *Celtic Heritage. Ancient Tradition in Ireland and Wales* (London, 1961), notes p. 381; IFC 102: 60-62 (1933).

15. Note: The Book of the Kings tells of how Moses had built one altar each for blessing and cursing at Mount Gerizim and Mount Ebal, the Book of Deuteronomy has Elijah erecting a cursing altar of stones. 1 Kings, 18.31-32; Deuteronomy 11.29; 27.

16. On Drumeland see Paterson, T.G.F., 'The Cult of the Well in Co. Armagh', in *UJA* 11, (Belfast, 1948), p. 128; on Tory Island see for instance Fox, Robin, *The Tory Islanders* (London, 1978), p. 9; Hunter, Jim, 'Tory Island – Habitat, Economy and Society', in *Ulster Folklife* 42, (Belfast, 1966), p. 40; Ní Mhorain, 51; St Clair, Sheila, *Folklore of the Ulster People* (Cork, 1971), p. 61; IFC 99:496-9 (c1928; I); IFC 472:455-61 (1938; I); IFC 1705:111-3 (1963/64; I).

17. IFC 109: 102-110 (1935; I); IFC 195:470-475 (1936; I); IFC 496: 119 (1937);IFC 810: 286-9 (1942; I); IFC 1140:44-7 (1935; I); IFC 1230:147-50 (1952;I); IFC 1242:180-2 (1943); IFC 1340:377-91 (1951-3); OSL Mayo (1838) I, 97-98; local information March 2001.

18. Logan, op. cit., p. 112.

19. Wood-Martin (1902), op. cit., Vol II, p. 55; IFC 1759:119-20 (Extract of *The Island of the Saints* or *Ireland in 1855* by John Eliot Howard, London, MDCCCV).

20. Otway (1841), op. cit., pp. 107-8.

21. Ó hÓgáin, Dáithí, *Myth, Legend and Romance. An Encyclopaedia of the Irish Folk Tradition* (London, 1990), p. 290; IFC948:232-3; S 96:181-5.

22. On Berenger see Wilde (1870-71), op. cit., p. 135; McGowan, Joe, *Inishmurray, Island Voices* (Sligo, 2004), pp. 147-8; OSL Sligo (1836), 15; Wakeman, W.F., 'Inis Muiredaich, now Inismurray, and its Antiquities', in *JRSAI* 17, (Dublin, 1885), pp. 233-242; Wood-Martin, W.G., 'Cursing and Healing Stones', in *The History of Sligo*, Vol. VII, (Dublin, 1842), pp. 381-3; Wood-Martin (1902), op. cit., Vol II, p. 64; IFC 1705:54-6 (1963/64). Note: One account from the early decades of the twentieth century is unique with regards to cursing stones in Ireland; it indicates that a curse could be lifted by turning the stones clockwise while blessing the victim of the malediction.

23. Cooper-Foster, Jeanne, *Ulster Folklore* (Belfast, 1951), pp. 118-9; Crawford, Henry S., 'Notes on Stones used as a Cure at Killery, near Dromahair, and on certain Bullauns', in *JRSAI* 43, (Dublin, 1913), pp. 268-9; Crozier, Isabel R./Rea, Lily C., 'Bullauns and other Basin Stones', in *UJA* 3, (Belfast, 1940), p.106; Evans (1957/1989), op. cit., p. 300; Kinahan, G.H., 'Cursing-Stones in Counties Fermanagh, Cavan, etc.', in *Folk-Lore* 5, (Dublin, 1894), pp. 3-4; Lowry-Corry, Dorothy/Richardson, Phyllis, 'Megalitic Monuments in the Parish of Killinagh, Co. Cavan', in *JRSAI* 67, (Dublin, 1937), pp. 162-3; Wakeman, W.F., 'Inis Muiredaich, now Inismurray, and its Antiquities', in *JRSAI* 17, 175-332 (Dublin, 1885); Wood-Martin (1902), op. cit., Vol II, p. 61; IFC 1807:17 (1972); S 962:111. Note: The sculpture by Seamus Dunbar is part of the Lough MacNean Sculpture trail.

Stones of Love and Fertility

1. Dutton, Hely, *A Statistical Survey of the County of Clare* (Dublin, 1808), p. 318.

2. Hall, Mr and Mrs Samuel Carter, *Ireland. Its Scenery, Character* etc., (1841-1843), Vol 1, p. 315. Note: A comparable custom was practiced in the western parts of Austria, and has recently been revived in several places.

3. S 576:78f, 80, 87; Local information (May 2005).

4. Burl, Aubrey, *Rites of the Gods* (London/Melbourne/Toronto, 1981), p. 189; for practice on the Continent see for instance Schmidt, Michael, *Die alten Steine-Reisen zur Megalithkultur in Mitteleuropa* (Rostock, 1988).

5. Danaher, Kevin, *The Year in Ireland. A Calendar* (Cork, 1972), p. 47; Price, Liam, 'Rock-Basins, or "*Bullauns*" at Glendalough and elsewhere', in *JRSAI* 89 (Dublin, 1959) p. 174; Westropp, Thomas Johnson, 'Notes on the Antiquities of Ardmore', in *JRSAI* 23, (Dublin, 1903), p. 375.

6. Burl, Aubrey, *A Guide to Stone Circles of Britain, Ireland and Brittany* (New Haven/London, 1995), pp. xi-xii.

7. MacNeill, Máire, *The Festival of Lughnasa* (Dublin 1962/1982), pp. 157-8; Paterson, T.G.F., *Country Cracks. Old Tales from the County of Armagh* (Dundalk, 1939), pp. 83-85; Local information.

8. Note: One exception in Irish tradition, and obviously a later adaptation of the basic idea, is the Treaty Stone of Limerick.

9. For a general description see for instance, MacRitchie, David, 'Notes on Holed-Stones', in *JRSAI* 22, 294-297 (Dublin, 1892) and Wood-Martin, W.G., *Traces of the Elder Faiths in Ireland: A Folklore Sketch. A Handbook of Irish Pre-Christian Traditions*, Vol. I (London/New York/Bombay, 1902), pp. 244-6; on the

destruction of the Stenness Stone see Grinsell, Leslie V., *Folklore of Prehistoric Sites in Britain* (London, 1976), p. 187.

10.   MacNamara, Fr Thomas V., *Guide to Holy Island* (n.p./n.y.), p. 33; Madden, Gerard, *Holy Island. Jewel of the Lough* (n.y./ n.y.), pp. 34-35.

11.   Ballard, Linda May, *Forgetting Frolic. Marriage Traditions in Ireland* (Belfast, 1998), p. 74; Evans, Estyn, *Irish Folk Ways* (London 1957/1989), p. 288; Evans, Estyn, *Prehistoric and Early Christian Ireland. A Guide* (London, 1966), p. 46. Note: It is noteworthy that into the early twentieth century, stones too played a role in wedding customs in the Mourne area of County Down. Newly-wed couples, holding hands, would run towards a particular stone, which the men had to kiss.

12.   Smyth, Daragh, *A Guide to Irish Mythology* (Dublin, 1988/1996), p. 163.

13.   Lankford, Éamon, *Cape Clear Island: Its People and Landscape* (Dublin, 1999), p. 12.

14.   On the importance of progeny in rural societies see Ballard, op. cit., p. 129; on eighteenth-century Ireland see Evans (1957/1989), op. cit., p. 283.

15.   Wood-Martin (1902), op. cit., Vol II, p. 247.

16.   Burl (1981), op. cit., p. 66; Dames, Michael, *Mythic Ireland* (London, 1992/1996), pp. 81-83; Dutton, op. cit., pp. 318-9; Grinsell, op. cit., pp. 40-43; Ó hÓgáin, Dáithí, *Myth, Legend and Romance. An Encyclopaedia of the Irish Folk Tradition* (London, 1990), pp. 161-3; Rees, Alwyn and Brinley, *Celtic Heritage. Ancient Tradition in Ireland and Wales* (London, 1961), p. 289; Wood-Martin (1902), op. cit., Vol I, pp. 348-349. Note: In Scottish and English lore the 'beds' would usually be caves.

17.   Paturi, Felix R., *Zeugen der Vorzeit-Auf den Spuren europäischer Vergangenheit* (Düsseldorf/Wien, 1976), pp. 145-146.

18.   Meehan, op. cit., p. ; 593-4; O'Hanlon, John, *Lives of the Irish Saints* (Dublin, 1875), Vol VIII, pp. 150-167; Wood-Martin (1902), op. cit., Vol. II, p. 70; local information (visit August 2005).

19.   Burl (1981), op. cit.213-4; Concannon, Maureen, *The Sacred Whore. Sheela, Goddess of the Celts* (Cork, 2004); Davies, O., 'The Churches of Co. Cavan', in *JRSAI* 78, (Dublin, 1948), pp. 116-118; Guest, Edith M., 'Irish Sheela-na-Gigs in 1935', in *JRSAI* 66, 107-129 (Dublin, 1936); Hickey, Helen, *Images of Stone. Figure Sculptures of the Lough Erne Basin* (Enniskillen, 1976/1985), p. 54; Hutton, Ronald, *The Pagan Religions of the Ancient British Isles. Their Nature and Legacy* (Oxford/Cambridge,USA, 1991/1997), pp. 311-314; Kelly, Eamonn P., *Sheela-na-Gigs. Origins and Function* (Dublin, 1996), pp. 44-45; on the historical background see Lydon, James, *The Making of Ireland. From Ancient Times to the Present* (London/New York, 1998), pp. 37-128; McMahon, Joanne/Roberts, Jack, *The Sheela-na-Gigs of Ireland and Britain* (Dublin, 2002). Notes: In France and Spain, comparable carvings of male figures outnumber the female

representations. In Ireland only two male exhibitionist figures are known to date: the first one stems from Aghalurcher Church, County Fermanagh, and is now preserved in the County Museum in Enniskillen; the second was discovered near Tomregan monastic site in County Cavan, and is today kept in Ballyconnell Church, County Cavan. The custom to take powder from the stone seems to be older, given that the Sheela-na-Gig from Seirkieran, County Offaly, today exhibited in the National Museum in Dublin, has holes drilled into the lower parts of her body.

20. On Gartan tradition see O'Hanlon, John, *Lives of the Irish Saints* (Dublin, 1875), Vol VI, pp. 279-280; on Tory see Logan, Patrick, *The Holy Wells of Ireland* (London, 1980), p. 82; visit to Gartan July 2005.

21. Doolan, Lelia, 'The sound of your footfall is as welcome as yourself', in Waddell, John/O'Connell, J.W./Korff, Anne, *The Book of Aran. The Aran Islands, Co. Galway* (Galway, 1994), pp. 238-239; on Kilquhone see Frazer, W., 'On "Holed" and Perforated Stones in Ireland', in *JRSAI* 26, (Dublin, 1896), p. 163; Macalister (1922), 52, Wood-Martin (1902), op. cit., Vol II, p. 240. Note: Around 1900, St Ciarán's Stone has been one of the most revered cross slabs on the Aran Islands. It was renowned for its curative virtues, particularly but not exclusively for female complaints.

22. Evans (1957/1989), op. cit., p. 283; Harbison, Peter, *Pilgrimage in Ireland. The Monuments and the People* (London, 1991), p. 69; Logan, op. cit., pp.82-83.

23. Note: Wood-Martin (1902), op. cit., Vol II, pp. 242-243, informs that a similar stone at Teampall na mBan, a short distance from the cashel, had been used in the same way. Island tradition, however, associates no rites whatsoever with this second holed stone. Logan, Patrick, *The Holy Wells of Ireland* (London, 1980), p. 82; McGowan, Joe, *Inishmurray. Island Voices* (Sligo, 2004), pp. 127-128.

24. Evans, Estyn, *Prehistoric and Early Christian Ireland. A Guide* (London, 1966), p.77; Harbison (1991), op. cit., p.210, and p. 219 on the symbolism of quartz; Hartnett, P.J., 'The Holy Wells of East Muskerry', in *Béaloideas* 10, 101-113 (Dublin, 1940); Logan, op. cit., p. 78.

Stones of Healing

1. OSL Clare (1839), 200-203; Westropp, Thomas Johnson, *A Folklore Survey of County Clare and County Clare Folk-Tales and Myths* (Dublin, 1910-1913), ed. Comber, Maureen, CLASP (Ennis, 2000), pp. 92-3; local information. Notes: Stone heads appear individually or in groups on ecclesiastic buildings from the Romanesque period until the sixteenth century. Folklore would usually explain them as the images of founder saints, or as manifestations of miracles. Their presence is clearly a concession to the ancient Celtic

veneration of the human head; it survived through the early Christian period and still surfaces today, when visitors touch or kiss the stone heads in order to have a wish fulfilled or a prayer for healing answered.

2.   Note: Accounts of telepathic healing are scarce, and it is reasonable to believe that they are merely incomplete renderings of the actual procedure.

3.   Hall, op. cit., Vol 1, p. 283; Westropp, Thomas Johnson, 'Notes on the Antiquities of Ardmore', in *JRSAI* 23, (Dublin, 1903), p. 378.

4.   Evans (1966), op. cit., p. 192; Logan, op. cit., p.105; Milligan, Seaton F., 'County Sligo', in *JRSAI* 26, 301-310 (Dublin, 1896), pp. 301-310; Wood-Martin, W.G., *Traces of the Elder Faiths in Ireland: A Folklore Sketch. A Handbook of Irish Pre-Christian Traditions*, (London/New York/Bombay, 1902), Vol II, p. 229. Note: The stone stands about 9 feet high and has an oblong aperture of *c* 3x3 feet.

5.   Logan, op. cit., pp. 24-5, 80-81; S 248:314-6.

6.   Wakeman, W.F., 'Inis Muiredaich, now Inismurray, and its Antiquities', in *JRSAI* 17, (Dublin, 1885), op. cit., p. 234.

7.   Rolleston, T.W., 'The Church of St. Patrick on Caher Island, County Mayo', in *JRSAI* 29, (Dublin, 1900); p. 358; Wood-Martin (1902), op. cit., Vol II, p. 106. Info August 2003, 2004.

8.   Note: In England and Wales, such homing stones would usually be megalithic monuments.

9.   Crawford, Henry S., 'Notes on Stones used as a Cure at Killery, near Dromahair, and on certain Bullauns', in *JRSAI* 43, 267-269 (Dublin, 1913); IFC 1744:223 (1967).

10. Wood-Martin (1902), op. cit., Vol II, p. 69; local information.

11. For Killerry see Crawford (1913), op. cit., p. 9; Wood-Martin (1842), op. cit., pp. 364-5; local information; for Waterford see Hall, Mr and Mrs Samuel Carter, *Ireland. Its Scenery, Character etc.*, (London, 1841-1843), Vol 1, p. 308.

12. de Paor, op. cit., p. 63; Harbison (1991), op. cit., pp. 191-204, suggests that these slabs might not necessarily mark graves; they could as well have been related to pilgrimage activities.

13. Rolleston, op. cit., pp. 57-8; Logan, op. cit., p. 73; visit 15.8.2003.

14. Wood-Martin (1902), op. cit., Vol II, p. 69.

15. Ó Danachair, Caoimhín, 'The Holy Wells of North County Kerry', in *JRSAI* 88, (Dublin, 1958), pp. 153-163; S 414:14-16.

16. 'Giraldus Cambrensis', ch. 63 in *Gerald of Wales (Giraldus Cambrensis), The History and Topography of Ireland,* ed. O'Meary, John J. (London, 1951/1982).

17. Di Martino, Vittorio, *Roman Ireland* (Cork, 2003); Crawford, Henry S., 'Notes on Stones used as a Cure at Killery, near Dromahair, and on certain Bullauns', in *JRSAI* 43, (Dublin, 1913), p. 269, dismisses their use for

mortars; Price, Liam, 'Rock-Basins, or "Bullauns" at Glendalough and elsewhere', in *JRSAI* 89, (Dublin, 1959), p. 161 supports the theory that bullauns were primarily made for baptism fonts and mortars. Macalister (1928/1977), op. cit., p. 170 suggests that the bullaun stones were a further development of the cup-mark motifs of the Bronze Age, and as such would belong to a pagan ceremonial tradition. Finally, Crozier, Isabel R./Rea, Lily C., 'Bullauns and other Basin Stones', in *UJA* 3, 104-114, (Belfast, 1940) suggested following a comparative study of basin stones from all over Ireland, that they can actually be assigned to two different groups: those created for domestic purposes and those which initially fulfilled a ritual pagan or religious function. Note: Bullaun (*bullán*) or basin stones are, strictly speaking, natural boulders of varying size, into which one or more round or oval depressions have been ground by human action. In Irish folk tradition, the term is also used when the impressions are of natural origin. The designation derives probably from the Latin word *bulla* for a hollow; the mystery of the provenance and initial purpose of basin stones has never been lifted.

18. Logan, op. cit., p. 108; O'Núanáin, P.J., *Glendalough or the Seven Churches of St. Kevin* (Wicklow, 1984), pp. 39-40; Price, op. cit., p. 168.

19. OSL Clare (1839), 172; Price, op. cit., p. 167; Westropp (1910-1913), op. cit., pp. 41-2.

20. Local information from well keeper and notice on site, 17.8.2003.

Stones of Spiritual Transformation

1. Note: The tradition of an annual Mass on St John's Eve has been revived in recent years; the former trust in the power of the stones, however, is hardly remembered in the area. Purser, Olive: 'Fragment of a Celtic Cross found at Drumcullen, King's Country', in *JRSAI* 48, (1919), p. 77.

2. Bremer, W., 'Note on the Holywood Stone', in *JRSAI* 56, (Dublin, 1926), pp. 51-54; Evans, Estyn, *Prehistoric and Early Christian Ireland. A Guide* (London, 1966), p. 212; Harbison, Peter, *Pilgrimage in Ireland. The Monuments and the People* (London, 1991), pp. 122-3; Orpen, Goddard H., 'The Holywood *[sic]* Stone and the Labyrinth of Knossos', in *JRSAI* 53, 177-189 (Dublin, 1923). Note: Carvings on large stones are exceptional. In Ireland a medieval version appears at St Laurence's Church in Rathmore, County Meath; the carving on the Hollywood Stone from County Wicklow is older, but impossible to date with any certainty. In Cornwall, carvings of the symbol were found on two rocks near Tintagel.

3. On Imbolc/St Brigid's Eve see especially Ó Catháin, Séamas, *The Festival of Brigit* (Dublin, 1995); for the Bealtaine assembly on the Hill of Uisneach see for instance Harbison, Peter, *Guide to National Monuments in*

Ireland (Dublin, 1979), p. 24; Macalister, R.A. Stewart, *The Archaeology of Ireland* (London, 1928/New York, 1977), pp. 308-9; for Lughnasa see especially MacNeill, Máire, *The Festival of Lughnasa* (Dublin 1962/1982). Notes: Bealtaine was concerned with cattle, which were driven through the fires for healthiness. Into the twentieth century, May Day traditions and superstitions were firmly connected with milk and butter. Lugh is known as Lugus in Gaul and as Llew in Wales. Samhain derives from the Irish terms *samh* for summer and *fuin* for end. The dates of the four festivals are based on the much later Julian Calendar which was only introduced in 1752.

4. McGowan, 123-5; OSL Sligo (1836) 15-7; Wakeman, W.F., 'Inis Muiredaich, now Inismurray, and its Antiquities', in *JRSAI* 17, (Dublin, 1885), 233-242; local information, visit August 2003 and 2004.

5. Bracken, Gerry, *The Inscribed Rock Outcrop and 'Rolling Sun' Spectacle*, unpublished, Westport. Local information on site (visit).

6. de Paor, Máire and Liam, *Early Christian Ireland* (London, 1958/1978), p. 62; Evans, Estyn, *Prehistoric and Early Christian Ireland. A Guide* (London, 1966), p. 87; Harbison, Peter, *Pilgrimage in Ireland. The Monuments and the People* (London, 1991), pp. 105-119 gives a beautiful description of the entire pilgrimage. Logan, Patrick, *The Holy Wells of Ireland* (London, 1980), p. 106. Note: Formerly cairns were also erected at the stopping places of funerals, on spots where someone has died, or on mountain passes, and the custom to add a stone to any cairn that one passes is common throughout Celtic countries.

7. Crawford, John, *Within the Walls. The Story of St. Audoen's Church, Newmarket, Dublin* (Naas, 1986), pp. 16-18; Dames, Michael, *Mythic Ireland* (London, 1996/1992), p. 154; Frazer, W., 'On "Holed" and Perforated Stones in Ireland', in *JRSAI* 26, (Dublin, 1896), p. 158; local information (visit). Wood-Martin (1902), op. cit., Vol II, p. 225 mentions a 'magical stone' called Shanven or the Old Woman; it was kept in a garden at Altagore, County Antrim, and occasionally presented with butter and oatmeal. Once, an ignorant mason removed the 'magical stone' and built it into a wall; the next morning it was back in its original position.

8. The Wishing Stone in the graveyard wall is similar to the English Plague Stones where, during times of epidemics, people left money in bowls of vinegar in exchange for food. It also resembles the holes in the walls, which were popularly used for ordeals in ancient Rome. Bett, 49-50; Wood-Martin (1902), op. cit., Vol. II, p. 249; S 1109:392; local information (visit June 2004).

9. Pettit, Sean, *Blarney Castle. The Story of a Legend* (Cork, 1989). Note: Dermot MacCarthy built Blarney Castle in the fifteenth century. His family held the estate until they were dispossessed in the aftermath of the Battle of the Boyne.

10. Note: St Brigid's Chair in Killinagh, County Cavan, for instance, is primarily known as a cursing stone, though it appears in later lore as a wishing chair; the Cailleach has seats at the Spellick, County Armagh, and Loughcrew, County Meath.

11. MacNeill, Máire, *The Festival of Lughnasa* (Dublin 1962/1982), p. 602; Ó hÓgáin (1990), op. cit., pp. 194-6.

12. MacNeill, op. cit., pp. 153-4; Wood-Martin (1902), op. cit., Vol II, p. 224; local information (visit 16.8.2003).

Christian and Pagan — Sacred Stones in Modern Ireland

1. Information leaflet on site; visit June 2005.

2. Note: Bigger, Francis Joseph, 'The Lake and Church of Kilmakilloge, the Ancient Church, Holy Well, and Bullán-stone of Temple Feaghna, and the Holy Well and Shrine of St. Finan's, Co. Kerry', in *JRSAI* 28, (Dublin, 1898), p. 320, noted the practice at Temple Feaghna in County Kerry. Abroad, the custom was once widespread and has been performed on stones of pagan and Christian connotations. It is possible that we have to look here for the original purpose of the cup mark decorations on megalithic monuments.

3. Local information; visit to Gougane Barra in June 2004, to Ballyvourney and Kilsarkan in August 2004.

4. Hutton, Ronald, *The Triumph of the Moon. A History of Modern Pagan Witchcraft* (Oxford, 1999).

5. Note: The movement shows a deep scepticism towards institutionalised monotheistic religions; thus, Pagans explicitly disassociate themselves from Satanism, as they consider Satan as a merely Christian invention.

6. Local information, visit August 2005.

7. The Janus idol is named after the bi-faced Roman god, but it was certainly not meant to represent the Roman deity. Scholars have dated both figures to times between the first and the seventh/eighth century AD, and interpreted them alternatively as representations of pagan kings or deities, or else as early clerics. Two-faced stone idols from Celtic realms on the continent are earlier. The oldest example known to date was found in Holzerlingen, Germany, and belongs to the fifth/sixth century BC; another figure from near Aix-en-Provence in France is dated to 122-123 BC. For more information see Di Martino, Vittorio, *Roman Ireland* (Cork, 2003), pp. 162-164; O'Kelly, Michael J., *Early Ireland. An Introduction to Irish Prehistory* (Cambridge, 1989/1997), p. 292.

Glossary

Aetiological – or: explanatory; from the Greek words *aitia* for cause and *logos* for word. Aetiological tales are stories that explain the origin of natural features.

Banshee – (Irish *bean sí),* literally 'fairy woman'. She is the supernatural death messenger of old Irish families, who announces an imminent death by wailing.

Bronze Age – began in Ireland *c.* 2,500 BC with the introduction of metalwork. The early phase of the Bronze Age overlaps with the late Neolithic and lasted until *c.* 2,000 BC; during this time, metal has gradually replaced stone as the major raw material. The Bronze Age might have lasted until *c.* 700 BC.

Bullaun – a stone with one or more oval or round depressions of artificial or natural origin.

Cairn – a heap or mound of stones, covering a megalithic structure. Cairns are also found at shrines, holy wells, mountain passes or stopping places of funerals.

Capstone – huge stone covering a dolmen or a megalithic grave chamber.

Court cairn – earliest form of monumental Neolithic tombs, built from about 3,800 BC. Some 330 court cairns exist in Ireland. They can contain one or more grave chambers, which are covered under a mound of stones or earth. The structures are distinguished by a semi-circular area or 'court' in front of the chambers.

Cross slab – a stone carved with one or more crosses.

Danes – term used in folklore to describe the Viking invaders of Ireland. The Viking period lasted from the late eighth century to the defeat of the Vikings in the Battle of Clontarf in 1014.

Dindshenchas – twelfth-century collection of older poems and prose tales which explain the place-names of Ireland.

Dolmen – from the Breton word for a stone table. Dolmens or portal tombs were probably a bit later than court cairns and consist of three or more standing stones, covered by one, occasionally two large capstones. Ireland has about 160 dolmens.

Fir Bolg – mythical pre-Celtic inhabitants of Ireland. Said to have come from Greece, they divided Ireland into provinces, marked the centre with the 'Stone of Division', and established the system of sacral kingship.

Formorians – (Irish *Formhóire),* a mythological race of giants. Myths show them as invaders or very early inhabitants of Ireland, who fought fierce battles against several other pre-historic population groups .The Formorian champion was the one-eyed giant, Balor.

Gaelic – term used to distinguish the language and traditions of the Celtic inhabitants of Ireland from the culture of the Anglo-Normans and English, who began their conquest of Ireland in the twelfth century.

Gothic – architectural style of the late twelfth century. Characteristics are pointed arches and elaborately decorated altar tombs.

Iron Age – began about 700 to 600 BC, when iron had replaced bronze as raw material for tools and weaponry, and ended with the introduction of Christianity in the fifth century AD.

La Tène – ornamental style of the Continental Celts of the last five centuries BC. The style is named after a bay in Lake Neufchatel in Switzerland, where a great deposit of Celtic artefacts was discovered.

Leabhar Gabhála Éireann – (short: *Leabhar Gabhála*) or the Book of Invasions of Ireland; a compilation of pseudo-historical texts which reconstruct the conquest of the country by successive groups of peoples.

Lughnasa – ancient harvest festival at the start of August.

Megalithic – from the Greek terms *mega* for large and *lithos* for stone; term to describe the massive stone monuments of the Neolithic and Bronze Age.

Milesians – or: Sons of Míl; according to myths the first Celtic settlers in Ireland. They came from Asia Minor and had to defeat the divine race of the Tuatha Dé Danann to gain possession of the country.

Neolithic – or: late Stone Age; from the Greek words *neo* for new and *lithos* for stone. The Neolithic may have lasted from *c*. 4,000 to 2,500 or 2000 BC. In the last phase, the Neolithic overlapped with the early Bronze Age.

Ogham – the earliest form of written Irish. Ogham was in use from about the fourth until the seventh or eighth century.

Passage graves – monumental graves of the Neolithic with a stone passage leading into the inner chamber near or at the centre of a cairn. Estimated 300 of these structures survived in Ireland, characteristically covered by round cairns and grouped into cemeteries on neighbouring hilltops or elevated places. They are possibly later than court cairns and dolmens.

Passage grave art – carvings on kerbstones or on structural stones of passage graves.

Pagan – the spelling 'pagan' is used to denote pre-Christian religions, while 'Pagan' stands for the modern spiritual movement.

Pattern – common term for a communal pilgrimage on a particular day. The term derives from the Irish word *pátrún* for patron saint.

Portal tombs – see Dolmen.

Rock art – carvings – usually of cup-marks, circles, spirals and dots – on standing stones or on the exposed surface of the grown rock.

Romanesque – style of architecture from the early twelfth century. Characteristic features are rounded arches and elaborate carvings.

Rounds – (Irish *an turas*) prescribed sacred journey between the praying stations of a shrine. The phrase 'doing the rounds' stands for making the pilgrimage.

Round tower – tall, window-less tower with conical roof and raised doorway which is only reached by a ladder. Round towers were parts of prestigious monastic sites. They were first built in the ninth century and served as lookouts and bell-towers. Due to their defensive capability, they were also used to store valuables during times of trouble.

Sheela-na-Gig – carving of a naked female figure that emphasises the genital area. The carvings occur on the walls of churches and castles; their initial purpose is uncertain.

Táin Bó Cuailnge – or: The Cattle Raid of Cooley; the story deals with the exploits of Ulster hero Cúchulainn and the fight between the provinces of Ulster and Connacht over the prestigious Brown Bull of Cooley.

Tuatha Dé Danann – or: The People of the Goddess Danu; mythical, divine inhabitants of pre-historic Ireland. They fought and defeated the Fir Bolg and the Formorians, but were later forced to submit to the Celtic Milesians.

Turas – see 'Rounds'.

Wedge cairn – structure from the transitional period between late Neolithic and early Bronze Age. Wedge cairns owe their name to the gallery of one or more chambers, which is wider and higher at the front. There are about 400 wedge cairns identified in Ireland.

Acronyms

AFM:	Annals of the Four Masters
AU:	Annals of Ulster
DIF:	Department of Irish Folklore, University College Dublin
IFC:	Main Manuscript Collection of the Irish Folklore Commission, DIF, Dublin
JCHAS:	*Journal of the Cork Historical and Archaeological Society*
JKAS:	*Journal of the Kildare Archaeological Society*
JRSAI:	*Journal of the Royal Society of Antiquaries in Ireland*
OSL:	Ordnance Survey Letters
OSM:	Ordnance Survey Memoirs of Ireland
PRIA:	*Proceedings of the Royal Irish Academy*
RC:	*Revue Celtique*
S:	Schools' Manuscript Collection, DIF, Dublin
Teathbha:	*Journal of the Longford Historical Society*
UFTM:	Material from the Ulster Folk and Transport Museum Archive, Bangor
UJA:	*Ulster Journal of Archaeology*
ZCP:	*Zeitschrift für celtische Phililogie*

Picture Credits

All photographs in this book are by the author.

The black and white drawings are taken from the following sources:

Page x   Westropp, Thomas Johnson, *A Folklore Survey of County Clare and County Clare Folk-Tales and Myths* (Dublin, 1910-1913)

Page xiii   Wood-Martin, W.G., 'Cursing and Healing Stones', in *The History of Sligo, Vol. VII*, (Dublin, 1842)

Page xv   Westropp, Thomas Johnson, *A Folklore Survey of County Clare and County Clare Folk-Tales and Myths* (Dublin, 1910-1913)

Page 4   Conwell, Eugene, *Discovery of the Tomb of Ollamh Fodhla* (Dublin, 1873)

Page 16   George Coffey, *New Grange (Brú na Bóinne) and other incised tumuli in Ireland* (Dublin, 1912)

Page 18   Conwell, Eugene, *Discovery of the Tomb of Ollamh Fodhla* (Dublin, 1873)

Page 36   Knott, Mary John, *Two Months at Kilkee* (Dublin, 1836)

Page 39   Wood-Martin, W.G., *Traces of the Elder Faiths in Ireland: A Folklore Sketch. A Handbook of Irish Pre-Christian Traditions*, Vols. 1-2 (London/New York/Bombay, 1902)

Page 52   Hall, Mr and Mrs Samuel Carter, *Ireland. Its Scenery, Character etc.*, Vols. 1-3 (London, 1841-1843)

Page 66   O'Hanlon, John, *Lives of the Irish Saints*, Vol VIII (Dublin, 1875)

Page 67   Chochrane, Robert, 'Notes on the Structures in the County of Cork…',in *JCHAS 18*, (Cork, 1912)

Page 81   Hall, Mr and Mrs Samuel Carter, *Ireland. Its Scenery, Character etc.*, Vols. 1-3 (London, 1841-1843)

Page 87   Hall, Mr and Mrs Samuel Carter, *Ireland. Its Scenery, Character etc.*, Vols. 1-3 (London, 1841-1843)

Page 96   Wood-Martin, W.G., *Traces of the Elder Faiths in Ireland: A Folklore Sketch. A Handbook of Irish Pre-Christian Traditions*, Vols. 1-2 (London/New York/Bombay, 1902)

Page 101   The drawing is by the author, Christine Zucchelli

Page 105   Conwell, Eugene, *Discovery of the Tomb of Ollamh Fodhla* (Dublin, 1873)

Page 110   Wakeman, W.F., 'On Certain Markings in Rocks, …', in *JRSAI* *13*, 445-474 (Dublin 1874/5)

Page 121   Westropp, Thomas Johnson, 'Notes on the Antiquities of Ardmore', in *JRSAI* *23*, 353-380 (Dublin, 1903)

Page 124   Wood-Martin, W. G., *Traces of the Elder Faiths in Ireland: A Folklore Sketch. A Handbook of Irish Pre-Christian Traditions*, Vols. 1-2 (London/New York/Bombay, 1902)

Page 134   Wood-Martin, W. G., *Traces of the Elder Faiths in Ireland: A Folklore Sketch. A Handbook of Irish Pre-Christian Traditions*, Vols. 1-2 (London/New York/Bombay, 1902)

Page 140   Westropp, Thomas Johnson, *A Folklore Survey of County Clare and County Clare Folk-Tales and Myths* (Dublin, 1910-1913)

Page 143   Wood-Martin, W. G., *Traces of the Elder Faiths in Ireland: A Folklore Sketch. A Handbook of Irish Pre-Christian Traditions*, Vols. 1-2 (London/New York/Bombay, 1902)

Page 147   Wood-Martin, W. G., *Traces of the Elder Faiths in Ireland: A Folklore Sketch. A Handbook of Irish Pre-Christian Traditions*, Vols. 1-2 (London/New York/Bombay, 1902)

Page 158   Orpen, Goddard H., 'The Holywood [sic] Stone and the Labyrinth of Knossos', in *JRSAI* *53*, 188-189 (Dublin, 1923)

Page 167   Wood-Martin, W. G., *Traces of the Elder Faiths in Ireland: A Folklore Sketch. A Handbook of Irish Pre-Christian Traditions*, Vols. 1-2 (London/New York/Bombay, 1902)

Bibliography

Ballard, Linda May, *Forgetting Frolic. Marriage Traditions in Ireland* (Belfast, 1998)

Best, R.I., ed., 'The Settling of the Manor of Tara', in *Ériu* 5 (Dublin, 1920)

Bett, Henry, *English Myths and Traditions* (London/New York/Toronto/Sydney, 1952)

Bigger, Francis Joseph, 'Cruach Mac Dara, off the Coast of Connemara', in *JRSAI* 26, 101-112 (Dublin, 1896)

Bigger, Francis Joseph, 'The Lake and Church of Kilmakilloge, the Ancient Church, Holy Well, and Bullán-stone of Temple Feaghna, and the Holy Well and Shrine of St. Finan's, Co. Kerry', in *JRSAI* 28, 314-324 (Dublin, 1898)

Bohan-Long, Rosaleen, *Stone Carvings of the Irish Iron Age* (Galway, n.y.)

Bourke, Angela, T*he Burning of Bridget Cleary* (London, 1999)

Bradbery, Jean/Service, Alastair, *Megaliths and their Mysteries. The Standing Stones of Old Europe* (London, 1979)

Brady, C.F., 'Some Observations on the Ogham Script', in *Teathbha* II, 124-133 (Longford, 1983)

Brady, Maziere W., *Clerical and Parochial Records of Cork, Cloyne and Ros*, Vol I (London, 1864)

Bremer, W., 'Note on the Holywood Stone', in *JRSAI* 56, 51-54 (Dublin, 1926)

Burl, Aubrey, *Rites of the Gods* (London/Melbourne/Toronto, 1981)

Burl, Aubrey, *A Guide to Stone Circles of Britain, Ireland and Brittany* (New Haven/London, 1995)

Carmicheal, Alexander, *Carmina Gadelica. Hymns and Incantations collected in the Highlands and Islands of Scotland,* Vol I (Edinburgh/London, 1972)

Chadwick, Owen, *A History of Christianity* (London, 1997)

Chambers, Richard, *White Island. History and Mystery* (Fintona, 2002)

Chochrane, Robert, 'Notes on the Structures in the County of Cork rested in the Board of Works for Preservation as Ancient Monuments', in *JCHAS* 18, 1-25 (Cork, 1912)

Coffey, Georg, 'Knockmany', in *JRSAI* 28, 93-111 (Dublin, 1898)

Coffey, Georg, *New Grange (Brú na Bóinne) and other incised tumuli in Ireland* (Dublin, 1912)

Concannon, Maureen, *The Sacred Whore. Sheela, Goddess of the Celts* (Cork, 2004)

Connolly, S.J., *Priests and People in Pre-Famine Ireland, 1780-1845* (Dublin, 1982)

Connolly, S.J., *Religion, Law and Power. The Making of Protestant Ireland, 1660-1760* (Oxford, 1992)

Conwell, Eugene Alfred, *Discovery of the Tomb of Ollamh Fodhla* (Dublin, 1873)

Cooper-Foster, Jeanne, *Ulster Folklore* (Belfast, 1951)

Corlett, Christiaan, *Antiquities of West Mayo* (Wicklow, 2001)

Cowell, John, *Sligo – Land of Yeats' Desire. History, Literature, Folklore, Landscape* (Dublin, 1990)

Crawford, Henry S., 'Bullaun Stones in the Glen of Aherlow', in *JRSAI* 40, 60-61 (Dublin, 1910)

Crawford, Henry S., 'Notes on Stones used as a Cure at Killery, near Dromahair, and on certain Bullauns', in *JRSAI* 43, 267-269 (Dublin, 1913)

Crawford, John, *Within the Walls. The Story of St. Audoen's Church, Newmarket, Dublin* (Naas, 1986)

Crawley, Ernest, *The Oath, The Curse and The Blessing* (London, 1934)

Crozier, Isabel R./Rea, Lily C., 'Bullauns and other Basin Stones', in *UJA* 3, 104-114 (Belfast, 1940)

Dames, Michael, *Mythic Ireland* (London, 1992/1996)

Danaher, Kevin, *The Year in Ireland. A Calendar* (Cork, 1972)

Davies, O., 'The Churches of Co. Cavan', in *JRSAI* 78, 73-118 (Dublin, 1948)

Dent, J.G., 'The Witchstones in Ulster and England', in *Ulster Folklife* 10, 46-48 (Belfast, 1964)

de Paor, Liam and Máire, *Early Christian Ireland* (London, 1958/1978)

de Paor, Liam, *Saint Patrick's World* (Dublin, 1993)

de Vries, Jan, *Keltische Religionen* (Stuttgart, 1961)

Dexter, T.F.G. and Henry, *Cornish Crosses. Christian and Pagan* (London/New York/Toronto, 1938)

Di Martino, Vittorio, *Roman Ireland* (Cork, 2003)

Doolan, Lelia, 'The sound of your footfall is as welcome as yourself', in Waddell, John/O'Connell, J.W./Korff, Anne, *The Book of Aran. The Aran Islands, Co. Galway*, 235-243 (Galway, 1994)

Dutton, Hely, *A Statistical Survey of the County of Clare* (Dublin, 1808)

Ellis, Peter Beresford, *Celtic Women. Women in Celtic Society and Literature* (London, 1995)

Eogan, George/Herity, Michael, *Ireland in Prehistory* (London/New York 1977/1989)

Evans, Estyn, *Irish Folk Ways* (London 1957/1989)

Evans, Estyn, *Prehistoric and Early Christian Ireland. A Guide* (London, 1966)

Fahy, E.M., 'A recumbent-stone Circle at Drombeg, Co. Cork', in *JCHAS* 64, 1-27 (Cork, 1959)

Ferguson, Samuel, 'The Burial of King Cormac', in *Lays of the Western Gael and other poems*, 54-9 (London, 1865)

Ferguson, Samuel, 'On the Ceremonial turn, called "Desiul"', in *PRIA* I, 355-364 (Dublin, 1879)

Fitzgerald, Walter, 'The Round Tower and Holed Stone of Castledermot', in *JRSAI* 22, 66-69 (Dublin, 1892)

Fitzgerald, Walter, 'The Kernanstown (or Browne's Hill) Cromlech, County Carlow', in *JKAS* 5, 339-343 (Dublin, 1906-1908)

Fitzpatrick, Elizabeth, *Royal Inauguration in Gaelic Ireland c. 1100–1600. A Cultural Landscape Study* (Woodbridge, 2004)

Foote, Peter.G./Wilson, David M., *The Viking Achievement* (London, 1970)

Fox, Robin, *The Tory Islanders* (London, 1978)

Franklin, D., 'Stone Circle near Glandore, Co. Cork', in *JCHAS* 9, 23-24 (Cork, 1903)

Frazer, James George, *The Golden Bough. A Study in Magic and Religion* (London, 1974)

Frazer, W., 'On "Holed" and Perforated Stones in Ireland', in *JRSAI* 26, 158-169 (Dublin, 1896)

Frazer, W., 'The Clandeboy O'Neill's Stone Inauguration Chair, now preserved in the Belfast Museum', in *JRSAI* 28, 254-256 (Dublin, 1898)

Freeman, A. Martin , ed., *Annála Connacht, Annals of Connacht* (Dublin, 1944)

Gerald of Wales (Giraldus Cambrensis), *The History and Topography of Ireland,* ed. O'Meary, John J. (London, 1951/1982)

Glynn, Fiona, ed., *A Sense of Carlow. A collection of Local Folklore and Myth* (Carlow, 1997)

Graves, James, 'On a Boulder with presumably Pagan Carvings at Clonfinlough, King's Co.', in *JRSAI* 8, 354 (Dublin, 1865)

Grinsell, Leslie V., *Folklore of Prehistoric Sites in Britain* (London, 1976)

Guest, Edith M., 'Irish Sheela-na-Gigs in 1935', in *JRSAI* 66, 107-129 (Dublin, 1936)

Gwynn, Lucius, 'De Shil Chonaire Móir', in *Ériu* 6, 130-142 (Dublin, 1922)

Hall, Mr and Mrs Samuel Carter, *Ireland. Its Scenery, Character etc.*, Vols 1-3 (London, 1841-1983)

Hamilton, Gustavus E., 'Two Ulster Inauguration Places', in *JRSAI* 42, 64-66 (Dublin, 1912)

Harbison, Peter, *Guide to National Monuments in Ireland* (Dublin, 1979)

Harbison, Peter, *Pilgrimage in Ireland. The Monuments and the People* (London, 1991)

Hardy, Dixon Philip, *The Holy Wells of Ireland* (Dublin, 1836)

Hartnett, P.J., 'The Holy Wells of East Muskerry', in *Béaloideas* 10, 101-113 (Dublin, 1940)

Heany, Paddy, *At the Foot of Sieve Bloom. History and Folklore of Cadamstown* (n.p./n.y.)

Henry, Francoise, 'Early Christian Slabs and Pillarstones in the West of Ireland', in *JRSAI* 67, 226-279 (Dublin, 1937)

Henry, Francoise, *Early Christian Irish Art* (Cork, 1954/1979)

Herity, Michael, *Rathcroghan and Carnfree. Celtic Royal Sites in Roscommon* (Dublin, 1991)

Herity, Michael/Eogan, George, *Ireland in Preshistory* (London/New York, 1977/1989)

Hickey, Helen, *Images of Stone. Figure Sculptures of the Lough Erne Basin* (Enniskillen, 1976/1985)

Higgins, Jim, *Irish Mermaids* (Galway, 1995)

Hollander, Lee M., ed., *The Poetical Edda* (Austin/Texas, 1962)

Hore, Herbert F., 'Inaugurations of Irish Chiefs', in *UJA* 1/5, 216-242 (Belfast, 1857)

Hunter, Jim, 'Tory Island – Habitat, Economy and Society', in *Ulster Folklife* 42, 38-78 (Belfast, 1966)

Hutton, Ronald, *The Pagan Religions of the Ancient British Isles. Their Nature and Legacy* (Oxford/ Cambridge, USA, 1991/1997)

Hutton, Ronald, *The Triumph of the Moon. A History of Modern Pagan Witchcraft* (Oxford, 1999)

Hyde, Douglas, *The Stone of Truth and other Irish Folktales* (Dublin, 1979)

Irwin, Liam, 'The Treaty of Limerick', in Jim Kemmy, ed., *The Limerick Anthology*, 230-232 (Dublin, 1996)

Jones, T. Gwynn, *Welsh Folklore and Folk Customs* (London, 1930)

Joyce, P.W., *Old Celtic Romances* (Dublin, 1978)

Kearney, Nicholas, ed., 'Introduction to Feis Tighe Chonáin', in *Transactions of the Ossianic Society* 2, 109-10 (Dublin, 1854-1855)

Keating, Geoffrey, *The General History of Ireland,* ed. O' Connor, Dermod (Dublin, 1809)

Kelly, Eamonn P., *Sheela-na-Gigs. Origins and Function* (Dublin, 1996)

Kelly, W.E., 'Inscribed Pillar-Stones, Co. Mayo', in *JRSAI* 27, 185-186 (Dublin, 1897)

Kennedy, Joseph, *The Monastic Heritage and Folklore of County Laois* (Roscrea, 2003)

Kinahan, G.H., 'Cursing-Stones in Counties Fermanagh, Cavan, etc.', in *Folk-Lore* 5, 3-4 (Dublin, 1894)

Knott, Mary John, *Two Months at Kilkee* (Dublin, 1836)

Lankford, Éamon, *Cape Clear Island: Its People and Landscape* (Dublin, 1999)

Lankford, Éamon, *Naomh Ciarán. Pilgrim Islander* (Cork, 2000)

Leask, H.G., 'The Long Stone, Punchestown, Co. Kildare', in *JRSAI* 67, 250-252 (Dublin, 1937)

Lee, Joseph, *The Modernisation of Irish Society 1848-1918* (Dublin, 1973)

Lett, Henry William, 'The Dun at Dorsey, Co. Armagh', in *JRSAI* 28, 1-14 (Dublin, 1898)

Logan, Patrick, *The Holy Wells of Ireland* (London, 1980)

Lowry-Corry, Dorothy/Richardson, Phyllis, 'Megalitic Monuments in the Parish of Killinagh, Co. Cavan', in *JRSAI* 67, 155-175 (Dublin, 1937)

Lowry-Corry, Dorothy, 'Cairns at Corracloora, Co. Leitrim', in *JRSAI* 67, 302-303 (Dublin, 1937)

Lydon, James, *The Making of Ireland. From Ancient Times to the Present* (London/New York, 1998)

Lynch, J.F., 'Lough Gur', in *JCHAS* 1, 289-302 (Cork, 1895)

Lysaght, Patricia, *The Banshee. The Irish Supernatural Death Messenger* (Dublin, 1986)

Macalister, R.A. Stewart, 'On a Stone with La Tène Decorations recently discovered in Co. Cavan', in *JRSAI* 52, 113-116 (Dublin, 1922)

Macalister, R.A. Stewart, 'Note on the Cross-inscribed "Holed-stone" at Mainistir Chiaráin, Aran Island, County Galway', in *JRSAI* 52, 177 (Dublin, 1922)

Macalister, R.A. Stewart, *The Archaeology of Ireland* (London, 1928/New York, 1977)

Macalister, R.A. Stewart, ed., *Leabhar Gabhála Éireann* 1-5 (London, 1938, 1939, 1940, 1941, 1956)

MacCulloch, J.H., *The Religion of the Ancient Celts* (Edinburgh, 1911)

McGowan, Joe, *Inishmurray. Island Voices* (Sligo, 2004).

McMahon, Joanne/Roberts, Jack, *The Sheela-na-Gigs of Ireland and Britain* (Dublin, 2002).

MacMahon, Michael, 'The Doughnambraher Font. Relic of an ancient Site?', in *The Other Clare, Journal of the Shannon Archaeological and Historical Society*, Vol 8, 17-18 (Ennis, 1984)

McMann, Jean, *Loughcrew. The Cairns* (Oldcastle,1993/2002)

MacNamara, Fr. Thomas V., *Guide to Holy Island* (n.p., n.y.)

MacNeill, Máire, *The Festival of Lughnasa* (Dublin, 1962/1982)

MacRitchie, David, 'Notes on Holed-Stones', in *JRSAI* 22, 294-297 (Dublin, 1892)

Madden, Gerard, *Holy Island. Jewel of the Lough* (n.p.,n.y.)

Makem, Peter, *The Cursing Stone* (Newry, 1990)

Meehan, Cary, *The Traveller's Guide to Sacred Ireland* (Glastonbury, 2004)

Milligan, Seaton F., 'County Sligo', in *JRSAI* 26, 301-310 (Dublin, 1896)

Newman, Roger Chatterton, *Brian Boru. King of Ireland* (Dublin, 1983)

Newry and Mourne District Council, *A Guide to Newry and Mourne* (Newry, 2004)

Ní Mhóráin, Muireann, '*Clocha Mallachta na hÉireann*' (unpubl. Ms, DIF, Dublin, 1979)

Nuttall Smith, G., 'Holy Well and Antiquities near Cahir, Co. Tipperary', in *JRSAI* 29, 258-259 (Dublin, 1899)

Ó Catháin, Séamas, *The Festival of Brigit* (Dublin, 1995)

O'Connor, Dermod, ed., Keating, Geoffrey, *The General History of Ireland* (Dublin, 1809)

Ó Crualaoich, Gearóid, 'Continuity and adaptation in legends of Cailleach Bhéarra', in *Béaloideas* 56 (Dublin, 1988), 153-178

Ó Danachair, Caoimhín, 'The Holy Wells of North County Kerry', in *JRSAI* 88, 153-163 (Dublin, 1958)

O'Donovan et al., OSL relating to the antiquities of county Carlow (1839), Cavan/Leitrim (1836), Clare (1839), Donegal (1835), Fermanagh (1834), Londonderry (1837), Louth (1835-6), Meath (1836), Mayo (1838), Sligo (1836), Tipperary III (1840), Waterford (1841), Westmeath (1837)

O'Donovan John at al, *Ordnance Survey Field Name Book of the County of Carlow* (Dublin, 1839)

O'Donovan, John, ed., *Annala Rioghachta Eireann, Annals of the Kingdom of Ireland by the 4 Masters from the earliest period to the year 1616* (Dublin, 1854)

O'Hanlon, John, *Lives of the Irish Saints*, Vols I-VIII (Dublin, 1875)

O'Halloran, A.J., 'Was the Treaty of Limerick signed on the Treaty Stone', in *The Old Limerick Journal*, 46-50 (Limerick, 1998)

Ó hÓgáin, Dáithí, *The Hero in Irish Folk History* (Dublin, 1985)

Ó hÓgáin, Dáithí, *Fionn mac Cumhaill* (Dublin, 1988)

Ó hÓgáin, Dáithí, *Myth, Legend and Romance. An Encyclopaedia of the Irish Folk Tradition* (London, 1990)

Ó hÓgáin, Dáithí, *The Sacred Isle. Belief and Religion in Pre-Christian Ireland* (Cork, 1999)

O'Kelly, Michael J., *Early Ireland. An Introduction to Irish Prehistory* (Cambridge, 1989/1997)

O'Meara, John J., ed., *Gerald of Wales (Giraldus Cambrensis): The History and Topography of Ireland* (London, 1951/1982)

Omurethi, 'Notes of Punchestown and Cradockstown', in *JKAS* 2, 37-46 (Dublin, 1906-1908)

O'Nualláin, Seán, *Stone Circles in Ireland* (Dublin, 1995)

O'Núanáin, P.J., *Glendalough or the Seven Churches of St. Kevin* (Wicklow, 1984)

O'Rahilly, Thomas F., *Early Irish History and Mythology* (Dublin, 1946)

Orpen, Goddard H., 'The Holywood *[sic]* Stone and the Labyrinth of Knossos', in *JRSAI* 53, 188-189 (Dublin, 1923)

Ó Riordáin, Seán P., 'Fragment of the Killycluggin Stone', in *JRSAI* 82, 68-69 (Dublin, 1952)

O'Sullivan, Sean, *Legends from Ireland* (London, 1977)

O'Toole, Edward, 'The Holy Wells of Co. Carlow', in *Béaloideas* 4/1, 3-23; 107-130 (Dublin, 1933)

Otway, Caesar, *A Tour in Connaught* (Dublin, 1839)

Otway, Caesar, *Sketches in Erris and Tyrawly* (Dublin, 1841)

Paterson, T.G.F., *Country Cracks. Old Tales from the County of Armagh* (Dundalk, 1939)

Paterson, T.G.F., 'The Cult of the Well in Co. Armagh', in *UJA* 11, 127-130 (Belfast, 1948)

Paturi, Felix R., *Zeugen der Vorzeit. Auf den Spuren europäischer Vergangenheit* (Düsseldorf/Wien, 1976)

Pettit, Sean, *Blarney Castle. The Story of a Legend* (Cork, 1989)

Plummer, Charles, *Bethada Náem nÉrenn/Lives of Irish Saint* (Oxford, 1968)

Prendergast, F., 'Ancient Astronomical Alignments: Fact or Fiction?', in *Archaeology Ireland*, Vol 16/no 2, 32-35 (Dublin, 2002)

Price, Liam, 'Rock-Basins, or "Bullauns" at Glendalough and elsewhere', in *JRSAI* 89, 161-188 Dublin, 1959)

Purser, Olive, 'Fragment of a Celtic Cross found at Drumcullin, King's County', in *JRSAI* 48, 77 (Dublin, 1919)

Rackard, Anna/O'Callaghan, Liam, *Fishstonewater. Holy Wells of Ireland* (Cork, 2001)

Raftery, Barry, 'Excavations at Killicluggin, Co. Cavan', in *UJA* 41, 49-54 (Belfast, 1978)

Rea, Lily C./Crozier, Isabel R., 'Bullauns and other Basin Stones', in *UJA* 3, 104-114 (Belfast, 1940)

Reden, Sybille von, *Die Megalith-Kulturen. Zeugnisse einer verschollenen Urreligion* (Köln, 1960/78)

Rees, Alwyn and Brinley, *Celtic Heritage. Ancient Tradition in Ireland and Wales* (London, 1961)

Renwick, W. L., ed., *Spenser Edmund: A View of the Present State of Ireland* (Oxford, 1970)

Richardson, Hilary/Scarry, John, *An Introduction to Irish High Crosses* (Dublin, 1990)

Richardson, Phyllis/Lowry-Corry, Dorothy, 'Megalitic Monuments in the Parish of Killinagh, Co. Cavan', in *JRSAI* 67, 155-175 (Dublin, 1937)

Roberts, Jack/ McMahon, Joanne, *The Sheela-na-Gigs of Ireland and Britain* (Dublin, 2002)

Robinson, Tim, *Stones of Aran* (London, 1986)

Roe, Helen M., 'Tales, Customs and Beliefs from Laoighis', in *Béaloideas* 9, 21-35 (Dublin, 1939)

Rolleston, T.W., 'The Church of St. Patrick on Caher Island, County Mayo', in *JRSAI* 29, 357-363 (Dublin, 1900)

Scarry, John/Richardson, Hilary, *An Introduction to Irish High Crosses* (Dublin, 1990)

Simms, J.G., *The Treaty of Limerick* (Dublin, 1961)

Service, Alastair/Bradbery, Jean, *Megaliths and their Mysteries. The Standing Stones of Old Europe* (London, 1979)

Smyth, Daragh, *A Guide to Irish Mythology* (Dublin, 1988/1996)

Somerville, Boyle T., 'Notes on a Stone Circle in County Cork', in *JCHAS* 15, 104-108 (Cork, 1909)

Spenser, Edmund, *A View of the Present State of Ireland*, ed. Renwick, W.L. (Oxford, 1970)

St Clair, Sheila, *Folklore of the Ulster People* (Cork, 1971)

Stokes, Whitley, 'The Prose Tales of the *Dindshenchas*', in *RC* 15, 278-336; 418-484 (Dublin, 1894)

Thom, A.S., 'The Stone Rings of Beaghmore. Geometry and Astronomy', in *UJA* 43, 15-19 (Belfast, 1980)

Toland, John, *A History of the Celtic Religion and Learning Containing an Account of the Druids or the Priests and Judges* (Edinburgh, 1815)

Wakeman, W.F., 'Three Days on the Shannon. From Limerick to Lough Key' (Dublin, 1852) in *Béaloideas* XI, 193-4 (Dublin, 1941)

Wakeman, W.F., 'On Certain Markings in Rocks, Pillar-stones, and Other Monuments Chiefly in the County of Fermanagh', in *JRSAI* 13, 445-474 (Dublin, 1874/5)

Wakeman, W.F., 'Inis Muiredaich, now Inishmurray, and its Antiquities', in *JRSAI* 17, 175-332 (Dublin, 1885)

Wakeman, W.F., 'On the Earlier Form of Inscribed Christian Crosses, found in Ireland', in *JRSAI* 21, 350-358 (Dublin, 1890/91)

Walshe, Patrick T., 'The Antiquities of the Dunlavin-Donard District', in *JRSAI* 61, 113-141 (Dublin, 1931)

Westropp, Thomas Johnson, 'The Cists, Dolmens and Pillars in the Eastern Half of the County of Clare', in *PRIA* 24, 107-130 (Dublin, 1902)

Westropp, Thomas Johnson, 'Notes on the Antiquities of Ardmore', in *JRSAI* 23, 353-380 (Dublin, 1903)

Westropp, Thomas Johnson, 'The Carved Boulder at Castlestrange', in *JRSAI* 17, 346-8 (Dublin, 1907)

Westropp, Thomas Johnson, 'Pillar-stone and Hole-stone, Co. Carlow', in *JRSAI* 17, 90 (Dublin, 1907)

Westropp, Thomas Johnson, *A Folklore Survey of County Clare and County Clare Folk-Tales and Myths* (Dublin, 1910-1913), ed. Comber, Maureen, CLASP (Ennis, 2000)

Wilde, William R., 'Memoir of Gabriel Beranger, and his Labours in the Cause of Irish Art, Literature, and Antiquities from 1760-1780', in *JRSAI* 2, 121-152 (Dublin, 1870/71)

Wilde, William R., *Lough Corrib, its Shores and Islands* (Dublin/London, 1872)

Wilson, David.M./Foote, Peter G., *The Viking Achievement* (London, 1970)

Wood-Martin, W.G., 'Cursing and Healing Stones', in *The History of Sligo*, Vol. VII, 360-367 (Dublin, 1842)

Wood-Martin, W.G., *Traces of the Elder Faiths in Ireland: A Folklore Sketch. A Handbook of Irish Pre-Christian Traditions*, Vols I-II (London/New York/Bombay, 1902)

Index